Low Pay -
Its Causes, and
the Post-War
Trade Union
Response

SOCIAL POLICY RESEARCH MONOGRAPHS SERIES

Series Editor: **Dr. Hans Wirz**
Department of Social Administration, University of Edinburgh, Scotland

Low Pay-
Its Causes, and
the Post-War
Trade Union
Response

Colin Duncan, B. Comm., M. Phil.
Lothian Health Board, Scotland

RESEARCH STUDIES PRESS
A DIVISION OF JOHN WILEY & SONS LTD.
Chichester · New York · Brisbane · Toronto

RESEARCH STUDIES PRESS

Editorial Office:
8 Willian Way, Letchworth, Herts SG6 2HG, England

Copyright © 1981, by John Wiley & Sons Ltd.

British Library Cataloguing in Publication Data:

Duncan, Colin
   Low pay—Its causes, and the post-war trade union
   response.—(Social policy research monographs; 3)
   1. Wage—Great Britain
   I. Title   II. Series
   331.2'941   HD5015

   ISBN 0 471 10052 8

Printed in the United States of America

ACKNOWLEDGEMENTS

This book grew from research I undertook at the Department of Business Studies, University of Edinburgh, into the general problem area of low pay. The period of research was funded by a grant from the Social Science Research Council. In undertaking the project, I was fortunate to be able to draw upon the considerable expertise of staff of the Department of Business Studies. In particular, I wish to thank Professor Hilde Behrend and Mr K.I. Sams for their helpful advice, encouragement and constructive criticism. I am also grateful to the many trade union officials in the central Scotland area who gave up their valuable time to discuss informally with me their views on the topic. The final script was typed with unusual care, speed and precision by Mrs Valerie Chuter, to whom I am also indebted. Finally, I owe an enormous debt to my wife, Linda, for her patience, encouragement and support throughout this project.

Responsibility for what follows, however, is entirely mine.

Colin Duncan
March 1981

'Low pay' is an elusive concept. For those whose pay is low and for
those, including trade unions, who would have such pay improved, low
pay is also a problem. Proffered solutions to the problem tend
naturally to be influenced by what are thought to be the causes of
low pay. In an admirably lucid manner Colin Duncan examines the
concept and possible causes of low pay and the trade union response
to the problem since 1945. The thoroughness of this examination
clinically exposes the complexities of the low pay issue and the
difficulties inherent in remedial action.

The selection of low pay as a topic for discussion suggests that
any author concerned has some sympathy with the position of the low
paid, however defined. Such sympathy entails the possibility that
emotion may hamper dispassionate analysis, clear judgment and the
development of sound policies to combat low pay. While Colin Duncan's
concern about low pay, especially as it relates to family poverty, is
apparent, it is not obtrusive. The analysis of relevant data and the
inferences to be drawn from it, is conducted with commendable
detachment. The author does not, for example, baulk at presenting
findings which appear to run counter to the 'conventional wisdom'
explanations of the causes of low pay. The discussion on inefficiency
as a presumed characteristic of low paying industries illustrates the
point. "The results obtained provide no grounds for assuming that low
paying industries are, in general, any less (or more) efficient than
other industries". Colin Duncan's approach is essentially one of
open-mindedness. While presenting opposing opinions he urges us to
concentrate on hard facts and hard figures and the reasonable
deductions that can be made from them however 'ideologically'
uncomfortable the consequences might be.

Having considered different definitions of low pay and made what I
think is the justifiable choice from among them, the author examines
the incidence of low pay in Great Britain and concludes that "low pay
appears to be a factor of major importance in contributing both
directly and indirectly to family poverty, particularly in families
containing children." It is therefore socially and economically
important to identify and evaluate the possible causes of such low
pay. To this end Colin Duncan assembles and examines with meticulous
care what might be called the literature on low pay of the post-war

period. Given the interacting nature of the possible causes of low pay, the conclusions drawn are, predictably perhaps, tentative. Even so, the differentiations of causality that are made, for example, between low paying manufacturing industries and low paying service industries are valuable in pointing to the need for possibly specific rather than general cures for low pay.

The contribution that the trade union movement can make to resolving the low pay problem is itself problematic. Low paid union members, like the poor, may always be with us. Better-off members of society may sympathise with the plight of the poor as may better paid trade unionists with their low paid workmates. However, harnessing the sense of goodwill in the trade union movement to do something effective for the low paid poses formidable difficulties not least because of the concern of particular unions about the preservation of differentials. The author brings out well the rather faltering development of TUC initiatives on low pay from the mid 1960s onwards when poverty was 're-discovered'. The role of incomes policies in relation to TUC policies and strategies on low pay is not overlooked. The author's overall assessment remains that "the policies and strategies pursued appear as yet to have made little impact on the problem." For Colin Duncan the issue of low pay is not simply one of poverty, the focus of TUC concern, but the reduction in the overall pattern of inequality.

The claim is made that "this study has sought to distinguish fact from fiction, clarify the main issues involved and provide further insight into the major dimensions of the problem." The claim is well founded. The uncompromising attention to the facts of the situation, the avoidance of polemic and the thoroughness of approach have produced a book which deserves to be read not only by students of industrial relations but by those who have any influence in shaping policy and action on the problem of low pay. It is to be hoped that Mr Duncan can carry the discussion further by considering in more detail possible cures for low pay while allowing, as he rightly does in this study, that the issues have to be placed in the broader context of other social and economic policies.

E.G.A. Armstrong
Robens Professor of Industrial Relations
Manchester Business School
April 1981

CONTENTS

TABLES

FIGURES

Editor's Preface

This is the third title in the series of Social Policy Research
Monographs. The first, "Teamwork for Preventive Care", deals with
interprofessional co-operation in the care of children, and in so
doing, touches on a number of important social policy issues. The
second, "Coping with Uncertainty" examines the strategies which are
employed at local level in the National Health Service when health
boards are required to allocate scarce resources in the face of
growing and often conflicting demands. The National Health Service is
a vital feature of the Welfare State, and Hunter's study is an
important contribution to the discussion on policy making and
implementation in this particular area of social policy.

The issue of Low Pay, which is the subject of this third monograph,
is central to the question of poverty in this country, the abolition
of which has been the concern of social reformers for long enough.
Rowntree and Booth in their pioneering studies in York and London
found nearly a hundred years ago that many families were in poverty,
not because of any contingency, such as ill-health or unemployment of
the breadwinner, but simply because the wages he was earning by
working a full working week were too low.

It is a strange paradox that this should still be so today, and
according to some leading commentators, the problem is on the increase,
if the number of those requiring Family Income Supplement is anything
to go by. The Low Pay Unit estimate that some 4 million full-time
workers earn wages which do not take them above the poverty line. If
the problem of poverty is to be tackled, the causes of low pay need
to be more fully understood. Duncan's study should lead to greater
understanding of one of the most central and apparently most
intransigent issues in the field of social policy today.

Editor: H.M. Wirz, MA, PhD, Department of Social Administration,
University of Edinburgh

INTRODUCTION

Few can have failed to notice an intensification of interest in the issue of low pay over recent years. The topic has attained a place among those more prominent social issues debated by governments, social commentators and trade unionists alike, and the term 'Low pay' now appears to have secured a permanent place in the vocabulary of industrial relations. What has prompted this interest? Has the position of the bottom wage-earners deteriorated in recent years, either relatively or absolutely, or may it be explained by a growing desire among trade unionists and others for a more egalitarian distribution of incomes and earnings? What in any case is meant by low pay and what is the extent of the problem? What are the causes of low pay? Have serious attempts been made by trade unions and other agencies to solve the problem and have they met with any success?

These and related issues have by no means been ignored in recent academic work, though in consequence of the breadth of the topic, information pertaining to low pay has accrued in a somewhat piecemeal fashion, with insights deriving from a variety of disciplines and evidence arising often as a by-product of other specialist fields of inquiry, notably from the work of the 'poverty lobby' and research relating to incomes policy. It would seem timely, therefore, to organise and build upon existing knowledge in addressing some of the more fundamental questions often posed about low pay. This study sets this as its task.

More specifically, the objectives of the study are presented as follows:

1. To provide detailed information on the incidence and pattern of low pay in Britain and on its relation to family poverty.
2. To explain the causes of low pay.
3. To describe, account for, and establish the effectiveness of, the trade union response to the problem since World War II.

In pursuing these objectives, the study adopts the following approach:

2.

CHAPTER 2 Attention is initially devoted to defining low pay. The definition adopted is then applied to current earnings data in measuring the extent of the problem in Britain and deriving its pattern by occupational group, industry and sex. Some consideration is given to the stability of this pattern. The final part of the analysis gathers together recent evidence pertaining to relation between low pay and family poverty.

CHAPTER 3 The discussion then focuses on the characteristics of low paying industries and, in a detailed statistical analysis, tests whether low paying industries differ from other industries in respect to a pre-selected set of economic and labour market variables. The analysis relies mainly on primary source data and extends previous work in this area.

CHAPTER 4 The results obtained are used as a basis for explaining the causes and current pattern of low pay in Britain. The link between characteristics and causes is discussed in the light of economic theory and previous empirical research. In so doing, the analysis assesses the adequacy of some well-established, and more recent, theoretical perspectives on wage determination and low pay. An attempt is made to account for certain characteristics of low paying industries and their relation to low pay through reference to developments in technology and economic structure.

CHAPTER 5 The focus of the study switches to a consideration of the trade union response. The discussion traces significant developments in union policy relating to low pay from 1945 up to the late 1970s, and attempts to account for the pattern observed by reference to economic, political and social developments over the post-war period. The trade union response is considered primarily at the level of the TUC, with particular focus on the interaction of government and TUC wages policies since 1945.

CHAPTER 6 Consideration is then given to the specific policies and strategies which trade unions have proposed or pursued since the mid-1960s in tackling low pay. This includes discussion of the main trade union conceptions of the problem and how these may be related to the ways it has been approached. The analysis seeks to identify the main weaknesses of policies pursued, thereby providing some insight into how the effectiveness of the response might be improved.

CHAPTER 7 The final chapter reviews the more important findings of the study and their contribution to a better understanding of low pay, and draws some general conclusions on the required direction of an effective trade union response.

1.   DEFINING LOW PAY

An examination of the incidence and pattern of low pay in Great
Britain must inevitably confront at the outset the problem of
definition. 'Low pay' is an equivocal term, reflecting the variety of
possible interpretations of what constitutes 'pay', and the differing
criteria against which pay might be judged 'low'. For example, pay
can refer to: basic minimum time-rates; earnings for negotiated hours
excluding overtime; or total hourly or weekly earnings including overtime. Various taxable and non-taxable allowances can be included in,
or excluded from, the definition. The criteria by which pay might be
judged low are equally diverse and can include: low in relation to
some notion of absolute needs; in relation to some notion of equity or
egalitarianism; in relation to what others receive in the same or
different occupations and industries; in relation to the effort, skill
and responsibility involved in the work an individual does as against
the work done by others; or in relation to an individual's contribution or worth in terms of profits or value added as contrasted with
that of others.
   'Low pay' can thus mean very different things to different people
and this poses obvious problems in selecting a suitable definition.
One possible method of overcoming this difficulty would be to choose a
pay figure which a majority of the population (say 51%) would consider
to represent low pay. This approach is particularly associated with
the work of Behrend who investigated people's views on low pay by
means of a number of national representative sample surveys conducted
in 1966, 1969, 1971 and 1973 which sought, among other things, to
ascertain the degree of consensus among the population at large as to
what pay level constituted lower pay. (1) However, such an approach is
costly and unless the survey dates were to be matched with those of
the Department of Employment's earnings surveys, it would be difficult
to relate a definition so derived to published data. Indeed, the
results of Behrend's surveys not only suggested that people's views on
low pay tend to be adjusted upwards with inflation but that the degree
of consensus on what constitutes low pay can also vary over time.
There was a much higher level of agreement as to the amounts which
represented low pay in 1966 than in 1973, when views were found to be

more diffuse, suggesting that a changing or accelerating rate of inflation makes it more difficult for people to make a judgement. (2)

A more common approach in recent studies of the topic has been to adopt, for convenience, and to ensure some consistency of method, one of a limited number of 'standard' working definitions which have become popular. These are discussed below in developing a suitable definition to be employed in the present analysis.

Working definitions are more commonly based on total earnings (usually weekly), including overtime, than on basic pay. For example, the National Board for Prices and Incomes (NBPI) adopted a criterion based on total earnings on the ground that 'basic rates exclude many elements which form a large part of many workers' remuneration such as incentive bonuses and merit payments' and that 'overtime pay forms a regular and important part of the pay of so many manual men in this country'. (3) The Board did, however, stress that the number of hours worked, especially long overtime hours, should be borne in mind when comparing earnings levels.

In identifying the level of earnings to be defined as low, working definitions usually rely on one of three standard criteria or 'cut-off' points. One measure identifies as low earnings those which fall at or below the lowest decile of a particular earnings distribution. A second measure takes, as the cut-off point, those earnings which fall at or below two-thirds of the median (or on some occasions the average) of a particular earnings distribution. A third popular approach sets the dividing line at that level of earnings which, after tax and cash benefits, would be sufficient to provide a family, usually consisting of a man with a wife not herself earning and two dependent children, with an income level equivalent to what a similar family would receive if the breadwinner were unemployed and relying on Supplementary Benefits. These three criteria were most frequently recommended as appropriate in evidence submitted to the Royal Commission on the Distribution of Income and Wealth, (4) and it is common for all three to be taken into account in arriving at a numerical definition.

Each of the above approaches has particular merits and limitations. It can be argued, for example, that the lowest decile and two-thirds median definitions pose an insoluble problem for policy makers and provide no fixed target at which to aim, since, in the absence of complete equality of earnings, there will always be some employees with earnings below these limits. However, in settling for the lowest decile approach, the NBPI viewed this as an advantage rather than a limitation of the criterion 'in that it underlines the relative nature of the problem: there always will be people who are low paid in relation to their fellows, and it would be absurd to suggest that the problem could be solved by (say) raising all earnings below the bottom decile to that level'. (5) The Supplementary Benefits approach on the other hand allows an absolute earnings target to be set and has the merit of relating the definition to an officially recognised standard of need. One criticism of this method, however, is that it embodies a number of assumptions regarding family size and circumstances which, while based on averages, are by no means 'typical'. The NBPI pointed out that out of $14\frac{1}{2}$ million families in the taxable field, only some $1\frac{1}{2}$ million consisted of a man and wife not earning and two dependent children. (6)

The earnings distributions to which the lowest decile and two-thirds median cut-off points have been applied have varied, as have the categories of employees subsequently identified as low paid by each criterion. Since the NBPI's study focused primarily on manual workers' earnings, the lowest decile limit was applied to the manual earnings distributions. Low paid men were identified as all adult men in full-time manual employment whose average gross weekly earnings fell below the bottom decile of the earnings distribution of adult full-time manual men, and similarly, low paid women as all adult women in full-time manual employment whose earnings fell below the bottom decile of the earnings distribution of adult full-time manual women. The Royal Commission also adopted the lowest decile criterion and applied it to the earnings distribution of adult full-time manual men. However, the Commission chose to define as low paid, all employees (men, women, manual, non-manual, full-time, part-time, adults, juveniles) whose earnings fell below this limit. The Low Pay Unit (7) on the other hand has consistently applied the two criteria to the earnings distribution for all full-time adult men (manual and non-manual combined) and defined as low paid, all full-time adult employees (men, women, manual, non-manual) falling below these points.

The differing approaches described partly reflect the differing aspects of the problem examined by the various studies, though some element of arbitrary choice would also appear to be involved. However, in developing a weekly earnings definition for 1974, the Low Pay Unit found it unnecessary to choose between the three major criteria, since the Unit's particular application of each to published data resulted in 'more or less' the same earnings figure. Hence the lowest decile and two-thirds median limits, when applied to the earnings distribution for adult full-time men, coincided in a weekly earnings figure of £30, a figure which also corresponded to that calculated as the Supplementary Benefits cut-off point for a two-child family. The low paid in 1974 were thus identified as all full-time adults with gross weekly earnings below £30. (8)

For convenience, and to ensure consistency with at least one popular approach, this chapter employs a working definition of low pay formulated on a similar basis to that chosen by the Low Pay Unit, and expressed in terms of a weekly earnings figure for a full working week. Since much of the analysis contained in the chapter makes use of New Earnings Survey (NES) data relating to April 1976, (9) the definition is formulated and applied as far as possible with this date in mind.

In calculating the 1974 cut-off point, the Low Pay Unit employed NES data relating to April 1974, and calculations were based on the earnings distribution of full-time men, aged 21 and over, whose pay during the survey period was not affected by absence. Applying the lowest decile criterion to the equivalent distribution for 1976 produces a weekly earnings figure of £44.50. The median of the same distribution stood at £65.80 in April 1976. Two-thirds of this figure equals £43.87. The two criteria thus result in cut-off points of £44.50 and £43.87 respectively in April 1976. (10)

The Supplementary Benefits cut-off point is more complex to derive. The calculation assumes two two-child families identical in all respects save that one comprises a male working head while the other relies for its income on Supplementary Benefits. The idea is to calculate the 'gross earnings equivalent' of the income level enjoyed by that family relying on Supplementary Benefits. The information below was obtained from the Low Pay Unit and the calculation is identical in methodology and assumptions to that submitted by the Unit in evidence to the Royal Commission, when suggesting an appropriate low pay definition for 1976.

The 'gross earnings equivalent' is derived by the following equation:

$$Yg = (S + R1 + R2 + W - F) + T(Yg - t) + N(Yg - F)$$

where:

Yg = Gross earnings equivalent (£s/week)
S = Supplementary Benefit weekly scale rates applicable to a married couple with two children in 1976 (£31.05). (11)
$R1$ = Average weekly payment by DHSS to claimants for housing rent in 1976 (£4.72). (12)
$R2$ = Average weekly payment by DHSS to claimants for rates in 1976 (£1.90). (12)
W = Average weekly working expenses (i.e. travel to work, working clothes etc.) incurred by a working man in 1976 (£1.75). (12)
F = Family Allowances payable to a two-child family in 1976 (£1.50)
T = Tax rate, 1975/1976 (0.35%)
t = Tax threshold for married man with two children, 1975/1976 (£31.40)
N = National Insurance Rate, 1975/1976 (0.0575%)

Substituting,

$$Yg = (31.05 + 4.72 + 1.90 + 1.75 - 1.50) + 0.35(Yg - 31.40) + 0.0575(Yg - 1.50)$$

$$= 37.92 + 0.35Yg - 10.99 + 0.0575Yg - 0.08625$$

$$0.5925Yg = 26.84$$

$$Yg = £45.30$$

The calculation thus suggests that the male working head of a two-child family would require to have earned at least £45 in April 1976 in order to provide his family with an income level equivalent to that enjoyed by a similar family relying on Supplementary Benefits. As in 1974 therefore, the three cut-off points result in a similar weekly earnings figure (£44.50, £43.87 and £45.30). On this basis, it would seem reasonable to define as low paid, all full-time adult employees (male/female, manual/non-manual) whose gross weekly earnings fell at or below £45 in April 1976.

As with all working definitions, the £45 definition has limitations. It fails, for example, to allow differences in the number of hours worked to be taken into account in assessing earnings levels. £45 per week is clearly worth more, in terms of hourly earnings, to those working 35 hours per week than to those working 45 hours. It is also inappropriate when considering the earnings of part-time employees where an hourly earnings definition is clearly to be preferred. Or again, to the extent that the low pay problem is viewed in the context of family poverty, it might be argued that a separate and lower figure should be applied to women, since women's earnings are rarely the prime source of family income. However, this distinction may prove inadmissible on other grounds such as equity or fairness, particularly in the light of equal pay legislation. These problems and limitations are borne in mind in the analysis which follows.

2. LOW PAY BY OCCUPATIONAL GROUP AND SEX

Armed with a definition, a suitable starting point in establishing the extent and pattern of low pay in Britain is to measure its incidence among the major employment categories (manual/non-manual men, manual/ non-manual women). Employing NES data, the cumulative frequency distributions of the earnings of full-time adults in the four employment groups were calculated. The results are plotted in Figure 2.1 in the form of ogives which show the percentage of adults in each group who earned below specified amounts. The data relate to 1976 and refer to employees whose pay was unaffected by absence. (13)

Applying the £45 definition, the figure shows that 8.9% of full-time non-manual men, 12.0% of full-time manual men, 51.9% of full-time non-manual women and 72.2% of full-time manual women were low paid in April 1976. In June 1976, the estimated number of employees in each of these groups was respectively 4.60 million, 7.80 million, 3.79 million and 1.72 million. (14) Applying the above percentages to these estimates shows that out of some 17.91 million full-time adults, approximately 4.56 million (25.5%) were low paid in April 1976, of which 0.41 million (9%) were non-manual men, 0.94 million (21%) were manual men, 1.97 million (43%) were non-manual women and 1.24 million (27%) were manual women. (15)

In considering part-time employees, an alternative hourly earnings definition is required. The equivalent of £45 in terms of gross hourly earnings is £1.05, this figure being derived by dividing £45 by the average number of hours worked by full-time men in April 1976 (42.7). It is not possible, however, to calculate the numbers and percentages of part-time employees earning below this amount, as NES hourly earnings data are presented in discrete units of 10p. Instead, a lower figure of £1.00 is adopted as the hourly earnings cut-off point for part-time employees.

Part-time employment is mainly concentrated among women. In June 1976, 38% of all women were part-time (1.89 million manual, 1.66 million non-manual) as compared with 5.2% of men (0.34 million manual, 0.36 million non-manual). Table 2.1 below presents estimates of the numbers and percentages of part-time adults by employment group whose gross hourly earnings fell below £1 in April 1976. The equivalent figures for full-time adults have also been calculated to provide

8. **FIGURE 2.1** Ogives Representing Percentages of Full-time Adults with Gross Weekly Earnings Below Specified Amounts – April 1976

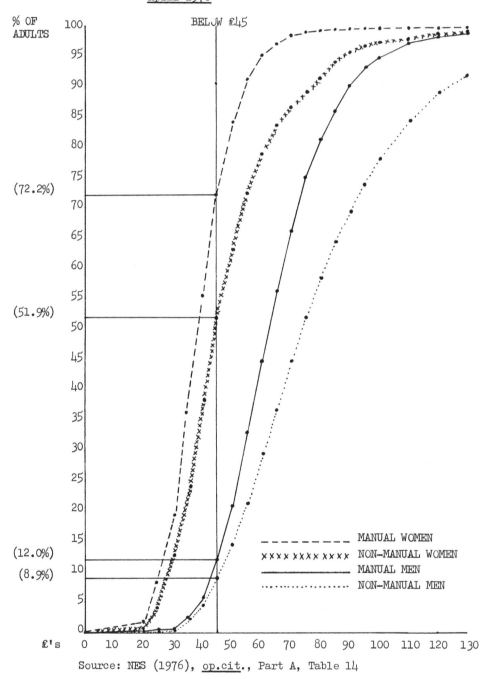

Source: NES (1976), op.cit., Part A, Table 14

comparisons.

TABLE 2.1   Numbers and Percentages of Adults with Gross Hourly
            Earnings Below £1 - April 1976

EMPLOYMENT GROUP	FULL-TIME		PART-TIME	
	Numbers (Millions)	%	Numbers (Millions)	%
All men (manual/non-manual)	1.08	8.7	0.39	55.6
Manual women	0.90	52.3	1.27	69.0
Non-manual women	1.15	30.3	0.84	52.5
Total (all adults)	3.13	17.5	2.50	60.4

Source: NES (1976), op.cit., Part A, Table 20, Part F, Table 175;
          Royal Commission, op.cit., Table M.7.

The figures suggest that the incidence low pay is more prevalent
among part-time employees than full-time. For each of the employment
groups shown, the percentages of part-time employees who earned below
£1 are considerably greater than the percentages of full-time
employees. Of all employment groups, low pay appears to feature most
prominently, in both percentage and numerical terms, among part-time
manual women. (16)

3.   LOW PAY BY INDUSTRY

In considering the distribution of low pay by industry, a distinction
may be drawn between industries employing relatively large numbers of
low earners and those where low pay is highly concentrated, that is,
where a high proportion of an industry's workforce is low paid. It is
possible that those industries with the highest concentrations of low
earners will also employ the largest numbers of low earners though
this need not necessarily be the case. The number of low earners
employed in an industry will in part reflect the relative size of the
industry's workforce.

The distinction is brought out in Table 2.2 which shows the
concentration and distribution of low paid men among the twenty-six
Industrial Orders of the Standard Industrial Classification 1968
(SIC 1968). For each occupational category, Columns 1 and 3 indicate
the proportion of each industry's workforce who earned below £45 in
April 1976. Columns 2 and 4 present estimates of the percentages of
all low earners of that occupational category who were employed in
each industry. Hence for agriculture, forestry and fishing, Column 1
shows that 40.7% of manual men in this industry earned below £45.
Column 2 shows that of all manual men in the economy who earned below
£45, 8.7% were employed in agriculture, forestry and fishing. (17)

TABLE 2.2   The Industrial Distribution of Low Earners: Men in
Full-time Work whose Gross Weekly Earnings Fell
Below £45 in April 1976

	MANUAL MEN(1)		NON-MANUAL MEN(1)	
	Column 1	Column 2	Column 3	Column 4
	% in industry who received low earnings	% of all low earning men in the industry(2)	% in industry who received low earnings	% of all low earning men in the industry(2)
All industries & services	12.0	100.0	8.9	100.0
Agriculture,forestry,fishing	40.7	8.7	14.6	0.8
Mining and quarrying	0.9	0.3	1.8	0.2
Food, drink and tobacco	8.7	3.2	7.8	2.5
Coal and petroleum	1.0	0.03	0.7	0.03
Chemicals/allied industries	6.4	1.5	2.7	0.8
Metal manufacture	2.8	1.0	2.9	0.6
Mechanical engineering	6.0	3.6	4.4	2.4
Instrument engineering	11.5	0.7	5.2	0.5
Electrical engineering	7.2	2.3	3.6	1.7
Shipbuilding and marine engineering	3.2	0.4	3.3	0.2
Vehicles	2.3	1.3	2.3	0.8
Metal goods not elsewhere specified	10.1	2.9	7.0	1.2
Textiles	15.0	3.6	6.6	0.9
Clothing and footwear	30.9	2.0	9.4	0.5
Bricks,pottery,glass,cement	6.7	1.1	7.8	0.9
Timber, furniture etc.	11.4	1.7	12.5	1.1
Paper,printing,publishing	8.7	2.4	6.6	1.9
Other manufacturing industries	10.9	1.8	7.7	0.8
Construction	8.8	8.5	8.5	4.6
Gas, electricity & water	1.5	0.3	4.1	1.1
Transport & communications	4.6	5.1	4.1	3.2
Distributive trades	33.2	15.7	24.7	29.1
Insurance,banking,finance	22.5	1.9	10.4	10.3
Professional and scientific services	24.4	6.7	7.4	14.3
Miscellaneous services	39.4	15.1	20.7	12.4
Public administration and defence	20.7	7.5	4.4	7.0

(1) Figures relate to men aged 21 and over whose pay was unaffected
by absence.
(2) Percentages may not sum to 100 because of rounding.
Source: NES (1976), op.cit., Part C, Tables 66 and 67.

Focusing on full-time manual men, Column 1 shows that out of the twenty-six industries, eight had higher concentrations of low earners than the all industries and services average of 12.0%. These were: agriculture, forestry and fishing; textiles; clothing and footwear; the distributive trades; insurance, banking and finance; professional and scientific services; miscellaneous services; and public administration and defence. Column 2 shows that in general, these industries also contained the largest numbers of low earners. While it is estimated that only some 25% (18) of all manual men in Britain were employed in the eight industries, Column 2 shows that together they accounted for over 60% of all low paid manual men. Over 30% of low paid manual men were employed in the two service industries, miscellaneous services and the distributive trades.

Column 3 shows that, in general, the industries with high concentrations of low paid manual men also had high concentrations of low paid non-manual men. The proportions of low paid non-manual men were above the all industries and services figure in agriculture, forestry and fishing, clothing and footwear, timber and furniture, the distributive trades, insurance, banking and finance and miscellaneous services. Column 4 shows that together these industries accounted for over 54% of all low earners though it is estimated that they employed only some 26% of all non-manual men. Large numbers of low earners were also employed in construction, transport and communications, professional and scientific services and public administration and defence, reflecting a high concentration of employment in these industries rather than high concentrations of low earners. In April 1976 these industries employed some 42% of all non-manual men though Column 4 shows that together they accounted for just 29.1% of all low earners.

As would be expected, NES data show that the industries in which low pay was most highly concentrated generally paid below average earnings. In April 1976, average male manual earnings stood at £63.3. In all eight industries where the proportions of low paid manual men exceeded 12.0%, average male manual earnings were below this amount, ranging from £50.2 in miscellaneous services to £58.8 in textiles. Similarly, for non-manual men, average earnings stood at £81.0 in April 1976 as compared with £61.1 in the distributive trades and £69.0 in miscellaneous services. Conversely, those industries with low concentrations of low earners generally paid close to or above average earnings. (19)

Table 2.2 also demonstrates the extent to which low pay was spread widely over all industry groups. Every industry contained at least some low paid employees. While in some industries, these represented a relatively small proportion of the industry's total workforce, (particularly where average industrial earnings were high), in sum, they were nevertheless numerically important. It is estimated that approximately 40% of all low paid manual men and the same percentage of non-manual men were scattered among industries which paid close to or above average earnings for these occupational groups.

Table 2.3 outlines, in the same format, the distribution of low paid women by industry, for those industries for which NES data were available. From Column 1, the highest concentrations of low paid manual women were in textiles, clothing and footwear, other

TABLE 2.3   The Industrial Distribution of Low Earners: Women in
Full-time Work whose Gross Weekly Earnings Fell Below
£45 in April 1976

| | MANUAL WOMEN(1) | | NON-MANUAL WOMEN(1) | |
| | Column 1 | Column 2 | Column 3 | Column 4 |
Industry	% in industry who received low earnings	% of all low earning women in the industry(2)	% in industry who received low earnings	% of all low earning women in the industry(2)
All industries & services	72.2	100.0	51.9	100.0
Food, drink & tobacco	69.9	7.0	65.5	2.4
Chemicals and allied industries	69.5	2.7	52.0	1.4
Metal manufacture	59.0	0.8	49.8	0.8
Mechanical engineering	54.4	1.9	70.1	3.0
Instrument engineering	64.1	1.6	68.4	0.6
Electrical engineering	58.7	6.2	63.0	2.5
Vehicles	35.0	1.1	41.4	0.8
Metal goods not elsewhere specified	68.1	3.5	70.9	1.3
Textiles	81.3	8.9	83.3	1.4
Clothing and footwear	89.2	10.9	84.6	0.9
Bricks, pottery, glass and cement	74.4	1.7	72.2	0.6
Timber, furniture etc.	69.6	1.1	79.4	0.6
Paper, printing,publishing	65.0	3.4	59.3	2.1
Other manufacturing industries	80.1	3.5	74.8	0.8
Construction	na	na	78.5	2.3
Gas, electricity & water	na	na	48.5	1.3
Transport & communications	32.3	1.3	34.6	3.3
Distributive trades	89.8	6.5	88.5	26.8
Insurance,banking,finance	na	na	60.0	11.7
Professional and scientific services	74.5	17.5	29.2	17.4
Miscellaneous services	81.2	14.7	61.2	7.2
Public administration and defence	60.2	3.0	40.1	9.9

(1) Figures relate to women aged 18 and over whose pay was
     unaffected by absence.
(2) Percentages may not sum to 100 because of rounding and the
     omission of a few industries for which data were not available.
Source: NES (1976), op.cit., Part C, Tables 68 and 69.

manufacturing industries, the distributive trades and miscellaneous services. While employing some 38% of all manual women, it can be seen from Column 2 that these industries together accounted for 44.5% of all low earners. Again, NES data show that these industries paid below average earnings, ranging from £32.6 in clothing and footwear to £36.3 in textiles, as against an all industries average of £38.1. (20) In addition, the proportions of low earners in bricks, pottery, glass and cement, and professional and scientific services were marginally above the all industries figure of 72.2%, though these industries paid close to average earnings.

From Column 2, the numbers of low earners were highest in professional and scientific services, miscellaneous services, clothing and footwear and textiles. However, the Table again shows the wide scatter of low earners among all industry groups. It is estimated that some 55% of all low paid manual women were scattered among industries with average earnings close to or above the all industries average.

For non-manual women, Column 3 shows that the highest concentrations of low pay occurred in textiles, clothing and footwear and the distributive trades. However, Column 4 shows that, excepting distribution, the industries with the highest concentrations of low earners were not generally those with the largest numbers of low earners. For example, professional and scientific services had the lowest concentration of low earners (and the highest level of average earnings) of all industry groups, and yet employed the second largest number of low earners. This reflects the high concentration of employment of non-manual women in service industries. While insurance, banking and finance, professional and scientific services and public administration and defence together employed 39% of all low earners (Column 4), it is estimated that these industries accounted for some 54% of all non-manual women in employment.

NES data do not permit a similar examination of the industrial distribution of low paid part-time employees. The previous section showed, however, that part-time employment was largely confined to women, and that a very high proportion of all part-time women were low paid. Those industries containing the largest numbers of part-time women are likely, therefore, to be those employing the largest numbers of low paid part-time employees. Royal Commission data show that in June 1976, part-time women were largely confined to service sector employment. 31.9% of all part-time women were employed in professional and scientific services, a further 21.0% in the distributive trades, 20.5% in miscellaneous services, 4.5% in insurance, banking and finance and 4.2% in public administration and defence. Together, these industries employed over 80% of all part-time female employees. (21)

4. THE PERSISTENCE OF LOW PAY

The pattern of low pay as outlined is that which existed in a
particular pay period in April 1976, but is not necessarily
representative of earlier periods. The extent to which the pattern
has changed over time, however, may be of relevance to an understanding of the causes of low pay and the likely effectiveness of
differing remedies.

A comprehensive examination of movements in earnings distributions
in Great Britain was carried out by the NBPI in 1971. (22) The
analysis focused on movements in the overall distribution of earnings
and in inter-industry differentials for full-time manual men, and on
movements in occupational earnings differentials for different
categories of male employees.

For full-time manual men, the Board's analysis suggested that the
overall distribution of earnings had remained 'remarkably stable'
over a considerable period of time. The evidence is summarised in
Table 2.4 below which also provides figures from the NES for later
years. While the Board warned that the figures were not entirely
comparable between years owing to minor differences in definition and
coverage, the Table nevertheless implies that very little movement
has occurred in the dispersion of male manual earnings since data
were first gathered in 1886. Expressed as a percentage of the median,
earnings at the lowest decile have remained virtually constant
throughout the period, and were only 1.6 percentage points higher in
1976 than in 1886.

TABLE 2.4   Dispersion of Average Weekly Earnings of Full-time
             Manual Men, 1886-1976 – Deciles and Quartiles as a
             Percentage of the Median

Year	Lowest decile	Lower quartile	Median	Upper quartile	Highest decile
1886	68.6	82.8	100.0	121.7	143.1
1906	66.5	79.5	100.0	126.7	156.8
1938	67.7	82.1	100.0	118.5	139.9
1960	70.6	82.6	100.0	121.7	145.2
1968	67.3	81.0	100.0	122.3	147.8
1970	67.3	81.1	100.0	122.3	147.2
1972	67.6	81.3	100.0	122.3	146.6
1974	68.6	82.2	100.0	121.0	144.0
1976	70.2	83.4	100.0	120.8	144.9

Source: 1886-1970 from NBPI (1971), op.cit., Appendix B, Table 1;
        1972-1976 from NES (1976), op.cit., Part A, Table 15.

Evidence considered by the Board also suggested considerable long-
run stability in the inter-industry earnings structure. A study by
Crossley, (23) for example, which compared the rankings of 132
industries ranked according to the level of average male manual
earnings in 1948 and 1959 had shown that only 11 industries changed

ranking by 25 places or more; that of the 20 industries that ranked lowest in 1948, 15 were still among the lowest in 1959; and that 15 other industries similarly maintained a position among the top 20. The coefficient of rank correlation had a value of + 0.87. The Board's own study produced similar results. Of 128 industries ranked according to the level of average male manual earnings in 1960, only 19 had changed rankings by 25 places or more by 1969. 12 of the lowest 20 and 13 of the top 20 in 1960 were still in the same group in 1969.

On movements in occupational differentials, the Board could not draw firm conclusions as available evidence related to differing occupational classifications which thereby distorted comparisons. However, there did appear to be some evidence for a long-run narrowing of differentials (1913-1960) between salaried professional and clerical-type occupations and manual occupations, and within manual occupations, both a narrowing (1885-1950) and later expansion (1950-1970) of differentials between skilled and unskilled employees. (24)

Overall, the Board concluded that there had been a remarkable long-run stability in the distribution of male manual earnings, considerable but lesser stability in inter-industry differentials, and, though the evidence was much less systematic, rather lesser stability in occupational differentials.

For women, data on earnings movements are sparse and little information appears to be available on movements by industry or occupation. However, the overall distribution of manual women's earnings, like that for manual men, appears to have remained very stable over long periods. Between 1938 and 1976, the lowest decile of the distribution of manual women's earnings, expressed as a percentage of the median, remained within the range 64.3% to 72.0%. In 1938 the figure was 68.3%, in 1976 it was 67.8%. (25)

As regards the relationship between men's and women's earnings, the NBPI again found evidence of considerable stability over long periods. Median weekly earnings of manual women, expressed as a percentage of manual men's, were 50.2% in 1906 and 50.0% in 1970, and in the intervening period had fluctuated within the relatively narrow range of 47% to 54%. (26) However, a later study which compared average earnings by sex over the period 1950 to 1975 found slightly wider variations. The results are summarised in Table 2.5 below which shows that while the relative position of manual women was broadly similar in 1950 and 1975, their position had deteriorated by as much as 9.7 percentage points in the intervening years. The figures in the Table coincide with the findings of an investigation carried out by the Trade Union Research Unit (TURU) on progress towards equal pay: 'Manual women's earnings as a percentage of manual men's have exhibited a tendency to deteriorate over the period since World War II to the late 1960s. Since 1969 there has been a slight improvement in the relative position of women. The improvement has not been particularly spectacular and only restores the position which prevailed in the latter half of the 1950s'. (27)

TABLE 2.5 Average Weekly Earnings of Full-time Manual Women as a % of Full-time Manual Men, 1950-1975

1950	1955	1965	1970	1974	1975
58.7	51.7	49.0	49.9	55.5	57.4

Source: Women under attack : CIS Special Report, Counter Information Services, 1976, p. 3.

It is likely that the relative improvement in the position of manual women from 1970 does in part reflect progress towards implementation of the provisions of the Equal Pay Act which became fully operational on December 1975, though it is difficult to predict whether this is part of a longer trend. Evidence prepared by the Low Pay Unit suggests however, that the legislation has had a more favourable impact on the earnings of women at the highest decile of the hourly earnings distribution relative to those at the lowest decile. Between 1970 and 1976, the highest decile of the hourly earnings distribution for full-time manual women, expressed as a percentage of the highest decile of the equivalent distribution for full-time manual men, increased by 11.3 percentage points. The corresponding increase at the lowest decile was 7.5 percentage points. (28)

It is only with caution that the evidence outlined may be related to the current pattern of low pay, bearing in mind that a number of the studies reviewed employed occupational and industrial classifications which differed from those of the NES. Nevertheless, the evidence does appear to suggest that the pattern of low pay in 1976 is fairly representative of that which has existed over long periods. While there has been some movement in occupational differentials, considerable long-run stability has been observed in the structure of interpersonal and inter-industry differentials. Differentials by sex have also remained relatively stable over long periods, though in recent years the ratio of manual women's average weekly earnings relative to those of men's has varied quite widely. Viewed from an historical perspective, the impact of equal pay legislation has been unspectacular and it is unclear whether recent improvements in the relative position of women represent part of a continuing trend.

These findings should not be taken to imply that there has been little earnings mobility on the part of individuals. On the contrary, NES matched sample data reveal that the composition of the lowest decile of earners alters considerably over short periods. Of all manual men in the 1970-1974 matched sample, only 2.9% were in the lowest decile in all five survey periods. (29) Nor do the results imply that the position of the low paid has not improved drastically in absolute terms. Between 1948 and 1970, average real net wages (for all employees) increased at about 2% per annum, (30) a figure which takes no account of the substantial increase in living standards brought about by the post-war expansion of public expenditure.

5. LOW PAY AND FAMILY POVERTY

Much of the recent concern over low pay derives from the widely held
view that low pay is a major, if not the prime, source of family
poverty. This view gained support from a series of studies dating
from the early 1960s which challenged the then prevailing view that
poverty had been eliminated, and purported to show that one of the
largest groups of families in poverty was that in which the prime
breadwinner was in full-time employment. (31)

'Poverty', like 'low pay' is an ambiguous and subjective concept.
Early attempts at definition and measurement relied on supposedly
objective measurements of the minimum amounts of food and other
essentials required to maintain physical efficiency. More recently,
subsistence measures of poverty have come under increasing criticism.
Townsend, among others, has argued that the level of minimum needs
required by an individual or family changes with the general standard
of living of a society, and that the fixing of minimum needs cannot
therefore be absolute or immutable. (32) Rather, poverty should be
viewed as a relative concept and be measured and defined in relation
to the resources available at a particular time to members of a
particular society.

In examining the link between low earnings and 'low family incomes',
the Royal Commission chose a definition of the latter consistent with
Townsend's concept of poverty. Families with low incomes were
identified as those whose incomes fell within the lower quarter of the
'equivalent net income distribution of families', thereby satisfying
the criterion of relativity. (33) In deriving this distrubution, the
Commission employed 'equivalence scales' to convert family incomes to
a common basis. These scales are essentially ratios of incomes
required by families of differing size and composition to achieve a
similar standard of living. For example, a married couple with no
children might be assigned a standard scale 1.0, a couple with two
children a scale 1.4, and a single person a scale 0.6. The equivalent
net income distribution is computed by dividing each family's net
income by the appropriate scale, thus deriving in effect a distribution of (supposedly) comparable family living standards. (34)

Employing data relating to 1976, the Commission subsequently
examined the size and composition of families in the lower quarter,
their main sources of income, and the distribution of low earners
(employing the broad definition noted in Section 1), among families
of differing income groups. The results of the analysis demonstrated
that the relation of low earnings to low family incomes was more
complex than supposed. The main findings are summarised below: (35)

(i)   the largest group of family units in the lower quarter of the
        equivalent net income distribution of families comprised the
        elderly (44%), followed by single adult families (28%).
        Families with children on the other hand accounted for just
        17% of family units in the lower quarter. However, in terms
        of the numbers of individuals affected, 60% of those who
        belonged to families in the lower quarter belonged to families
        with children and only some 30% belonged to elderly family
        units;

(ii)   57% of the lower quarter of family units did not contain an earner. In aggregate, families in the lower quarter derived some 50% of gross income from employment, 40% from state benefits and the remaining 10% from a variety of other sources (gifts, private pension schemes etc.). Elderly families derived about 90% of gross income from state benefits while families with children derived between 51% and 76% of gross income (varying with family size) from employment;

(iii) of all earners in family units in the lower quarter, some 80% had earnings below the bottom decile. By contrast, of all earners in family units in the top three-quarters of the equivalent net income distribution, only 40% had earnings below the bottom decile;

(iv)   on the other hand, only some 20% of all earners with earnings below the bottom decile belonged to family units in the lower quarter.

The Commission interpreted these results as implying that low earnings were a major source of low incomes or family poverty only in families containing children. The major source of income in low income families with children was derived from earnings (item (ii)), and the majority of earners in these families were low paid (item (iii)). While families with children represented a minority of all family units in the lower quarter, they nevertheless accounted for the largest number of individuals belonging to low income families (item (i)). The final result (item (iv)) might be viewed as somewhat surprising, though it is to be remembered that 'low earners' was defined widely to include juveniles, part-timers and women. It is likely that a high proportion of these groups do not provide the main source of family income, but rather supplement the earnings of other family members. The Commission interpreted the result as suggesting that working women in particular had been responsible for lifting a large number of families out of the lower income bracket.

In addition to its direct relation to low incomes in families with children, evidence suggests that low pay can also diminish the capacity of these families to improve their living standards and escape from the lower income bracket. This more indirect consequence of low pay arises from the operation of what has become popularly labelled 'the poverty trap'.

The poverty trap refers to the potentially unfavourable interaction of low earnings, taxes and welfare benefits in families with children. This occurs because the range of earnings which attracts Family Income Supplement (FIS), (36) rent and rate rebates, free school meals and welfare milk overlaps the range for which income tax is payable. Since these benefits are means-tested, and diminish or are cut off when earnings increase, some families receiving means-tested benefits may find that an increase in earnings is wholly or substantially offset by a reduction in their means-tested benefits, together with increases in their income tax and national insurance contributions, so that over a wide range of lower earnings, the family's income would be at much the same level.

The possible effects of the poverty trap on a two-child family in July 1976 are illustrated graphically in Figure 2.2 which shows the

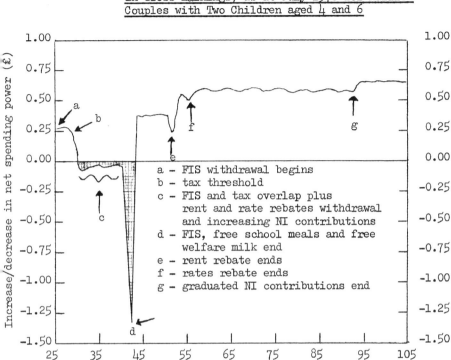

FIGURE 2.2   Differences in Net Spending Power for a £1 Increase in Gross Earnings, as at July 1976 for Married Couples with Two Children aged 4 and 6

a – FIS withdrawal begins
b – tax threshold
c – FIS and tax overlap plus rent and rate rebates withdrawal and increasing NI contributions
d – FIS, free school meals and free welfare milk end
e – rent rebate ends
f – rates rebate ends
g – graduated NI contributions end

Source: Social Trends No. 7, 1976, HMSO, 1976

Notes:
1. The figure relies on the following assumptions: the family is a hypothetical one, living in typical accommodation; rent of £4.72 and rates of £1.90 are assumed; it is also assumed that the gross income of the family is earned solely by the husband, who has work expenses of £1.75 per week; and it is assumed that all benefits are adjusted immediately upon receipt of a pay rise.
2. Net spending power is defined as gross weekly earnings plus benefits (family allowances, FIS, rates rebates, rent rebates, free school meals and free welfare milk) less tax (income tax and national insurance) less gross housing costs (rent and rates) less work expenses.

marginal net benefit, in terms of net spending power, (or in effect the marginal net 'tax'), of each additional pound received in earnings by the husband. The figure shows that even at the lowest levels of earnings, an increase in pay yields very little net benefit. On £25, FIS payment has begun to decline so that a £1 increase in pay yields a net increase in family spending power of just 25p. The horizontal line in the diagram represents the cut-off point below which increases in gross earnings represent an actual decline in family spending power. Hence, within the earnings band at 'c', the joint effects of taxation, national insurance and further withdrawal of FIS, rent and rates rebates means that an increase in earnings yields a reduction in family living standards. The position is worst at 'd' where, as a consequence of the further withdrawal of free school meals and welfare milk, a £1 increase on earnings of around £40 reduces family spending power by approximately £1.30. Not until the husbands earnings reach £55 per week do the family gain more than 50p out of each extra pound earned.

The DHSS have estimated the number of families potentially in the poverty trap at about 50,000. This figure referred to those families in 1975, with and without children, whose net spending power could decline if earnings were increased. An additional 40,000 families would retain less than 25p of a £1 increase in earnings and a further 200,000 would retain less than 50p. (37) Evidence prepared by the Low Pay Unit suggests that these numbers have increased considerably since 1975. Pond has shown that over the period 1974-79, the earnings band over which families can receive the major means-tested benefits and at the same time pay tax had approximately doubled in width. (38)

While acknowledging the detrimental influence of the poverty trap on families with children, the Royal Commission argued that its effects were more serious in theory than in practice. In particular it was argued that FIS and other benefits, contrary to what is assumed in Figure 2.2, are awarded for fixed periods, usually 12 months, and so are not withdrawn immediately a family's earnings increase. Hence in practice, increases in family earnings do not necessarily exclude reasonable increases in net disposable income. This view was challenged by the Low Pay Unit who argued that faith in the 12 month rule as a solution to the trap relied on 'a remarkable coincidence of dates', including dates of pay awards, dates of application for benefits and dates of uprating. Case studies of a number of families affected suggested that the practical effects of the trap were very close to those predicted in theory. (39)

It has further been argued that the link between low pay and family poverty is strengthened through the differential effects of inflation. The living standards of low earners and their families, it is argued, are more seriously eroded by the impact of inflation than are the living standards of higher income groups. This occurs because different income groups have different expenditure patterns: low earners and their families spend a higher proportion of their incomes on necessities such as food, housing, fuel and light than do higher income groups; and because these items tend to increase in price at a faster rate than do items which figure more prominently in the household budgets of higher income groups, (for example consumer durables),

the percentage increase in the cost of living for low earners and
their families is greater than for higher income groups.

Evidence prepared by the Low Pay Unit appears to support this
argument. From the Family Expenditure Survey (FES) 1973, it was
estimated that in those households at the lower decile of the income
distribution of households (40) (non-adjusted by equivalence scales),
housing on average accounted for 14.2% of all household expenditure,
fuel and light 6.1% and food a further 28.8% as compared with 12.5%,
5.3% and 23.1% respectively in households in the highest decile. On
the other hand, it was estimated from the Retail Price Index (RPI)
that between January 1970 and January 1974, the price of food had
risen by 61%, fuel and light by 30% and the cost of housing had
increased on average by nearly 50%. By contrast, durable household
goods registered price increases of 29% over the same period. (41)

More recently, the Low Pay Unit and the Civil and Public Services
Association jointly constructed and published a 'Low Paid Price
Index' (LPPI) as a rival indicator to the RPI in measuring cost of
living changes for low earners and their families. The LPPI was
designed to measure cost of living changes for households whose main
source of income derives from a single wage earner with earnings
falling within the lowest decile of the earnings distribution of
full-time men (manual and non-manual). It was found that the average
household income of these households fell within the lower quarter of
the income distribution of all households (non-adjusted by equivalence
scales). In constructing the new index, orthodox RPI weightings on
certain items were readjusted, on the basis of FES data, so as to
reflect more accurately the expenditure patterns of these low earning
households.

The results of the new index showed that between January 1974 and
April 1978, the cost of living, as measured by the LPPI, had risen
4.6 percentage points above the increase recorded by the RPI over the
same period. By contrast, an index constructed on a similar basis for
households in the top income decile recorded increases broadly similar
to those recorded by the RPI. (42)

Finally, it has been argued that low pay is associated with a more
general pattern of social and labour market disadvantage which has an
important influence on family living standards. Some of the social
implications of low pay were highlighted by Coates and Silburn in a
survey of earnings and poverty in St Annes, Nottingham. The low paid,
the authors observed, 'are herded together in ghettos, in which they
share not only low wages, but a dozen other social deprivations, from
slum houses, meagre public services, squalid urban surroundings, at
the material level: to the accompanying moral sense that nothing can
be done, that they are at the bottom of the pit'. (43)

Within the labour market, evidence produced by Atkinson showed that
in comparison with higher paid employees, lower paid manual men
generally experienced higher levels of unemployment and job in-
security, higher rates of sickness and absence, were less likely to
receive fringe benefits or belong to occupational pension schemes,
and where they did belong to these schemes or receive fringe benefits,
payments were below average. (44)

It is unclear whether a number of these labour market associations
(sickness, absence, high labour turnover) are consequences of the

conditions of low paid occupations, or whether causality is in the other direction, that high absence and sickness rates and other personal characteristics of certain individuals largely confine their employment opportunities to low paid occupations and industries. Whatever the reason, Atkinson suggests that in association with low earnings, these factors further contribute to family poverty, not only in the short term, but throughout different stages in the family's 'life cycle'. For example, low earnings and the frequent interruption or loss of earnings curtails a family's ability to save or to invest in a housing mortgage. This, in conjunction with factors such as the absence of private pension schemes, forces primary reliance on state benefits in old age which, as Royal Commission data suggest, are insufficient to prevent family poverty.

6.   SUMMARY AND CONCLUSIONS

1.   The extent of the problem   As defined and measured according to conventional criteria, low pay is a large and serious problem in Great Britain. In April 1976, over a quarter of all full-time adults had weekly earnings below £45 and over 60% of all part-time adults had hourly earnings below £1.

2.   By occupational group and sex   The problem is very much greater among women than men. For both sexes, a higher proportion of manual employees are low paid than are non-manual, and a higher proportion of part-time employees are low paid than are full-time. Of all employment groups, the problem is most prominent in both numerical and percentage terms among part-time manual women.

3.   By industry   The industrial pattern of low pay differs by employment group (manual/non-manual men, manual/non-manual women) though some similarities in pattern were observed. In the non-manufacturing sector, the highest concentrations of low pay generally occurred in textiles, clothing and footwear industries. In the non-manufacturing sectors, agriculture, miscellaneous services and distribution had particularly high concentrations of low earners. Industries with high concentrations of low earners generally paid below average earnings. Numerically, low pay was more pronounced in service industries, reflecting the high concentration of employment in these industries, particularly among part-time workers and non-manual women. Low paid employees were nevertheless scattered widely over all industries.

4.   The persistence of low pay   The pattern of low pay in 1976 appears to be largely representative of that which has existed over long periods.

5.   Low pay and family poverty   Low pay appears to be a factor of major importance in contributing both directly and indirectly to family poverty, particularly in families containing children.

CHARACTERISTICS OF LOW PAYING INDUSTRIES

1. OBJECTIVES AND METHODOLOGY

It has been shown that low pay is relatively more serious in particular industries and services. An examination of some of the characteristics of low paying industries may thus afford some understanding of the causes of low pay.

Given the diversity of low paying industries, however, this may seem a daunting task. Indeed, the dissimilarity of these industries has been emphasised in recent case studies of the problem, where low pay has been found to be associated with characteristics or combinations of characteristics largely peculiar to individual industries. In examining the causes of low pay in the NHS, laundries and the contract cleaning industry, for example, the NBPI were unable to draw firm general conclusions:

'We find that very different factors combine in each of our reference industries to produce low pay. An obvious common factor is the fairly low general level of skill and capacity expected of, and possessed by the workers concerned. But many other factors are very different, for example, the market environment, the structure, organisation and skills of management, the degree of trade union organisation and effectiveness, and the arrangements for fixing wages'. (1)

While accepting these differences, this chapter seeks to locate broad similarities in low paying industries which may be important to an understanding of the problem and which may not be apparent from the results of a limited number of case studies. The approach adopted is similar to that employed in a pioneering study of low paying industries undertaken by Marquand in 1967. (2) Employing 1960 earnings data, Marquand tested whether low paying industries, relative to other industries, were more strongly characterised by factors thought to weaken bargaining strength. Variables examined included: the size of firms comprising industries; skill levels of employees by industry; industrial employment trends; sex ratios by industry; and certain 'institutional factors' relating to industrial earnings structures and the forms of collective bargaining machinery in operation.

Owing to limitations of data, however, Marquand's study was largely confined to the manufacturing sector. On the basis of more recent earnings data, the present analysis includes consideration of the service sector (3) where the problem appears to be most serious, and extends the list of variables considered by Marquand to include comparisons of trade union density levels by industry, industrial trends in productivity and output, and, since low pay is often ascribed to inefficiency, the relative efficiency of low paying industries is also examined.

The industrial pattern of low pay was found to vary for the different employment groups examined in the previous chapter. For this reason, it is not possible to specify, for the purposes of the analysis, a single group of industries which may be defined as 'low paying' for all major employment categories, whether the criterion of low paying be in terms of concentrations of low earners by industry, numbers of low earners by industry or average industrial earnings. Moreover, omissions in NES data prevent aggregation of industrial earnings data over differing occupational groups, so that it is not possible to estimate, for example, average industrial earnings in respect of all employees in an industry, or the proportion of an industry's total workforce who earned below specified amounts.

To avoid undue complexity, therefore, low paying industries are identified by reference to one employment group only, as those Industrial Orders of SIC 1968 which had the lowest level of average gross weekly earnings for full-time manual men in April 1976. The nine lowest paying industries by this criterion are listed in Table 3.1. Also included in the Table is the Order 'Leather, leather goods and fur', a group of industries not covered in the NES sample but which, from Census of Production data relating to 1972, was found to have the second lowest level of average male manual earnings of all manufacturing industries. (4) A breakdown of these ten Orders into their component Minimum List Headings is contained in Appendix 3.1.

Apart from considerations of expediency, this approach was considered most appropriate on the following additional grounds:

(i)   it broadly coincides with the method adopted by Marquand, who chose to define as low paying industries those in which earnings at the lowest decile of the male manual earnings distribution were lowest. The choice of the lowest decile (as opposed to the mean) does not represent a major point of departure. If the Industrial Orders in the 1976 NES are ranked according to the earnings of male manual employees at the lowest decile, the nine lowest paying industries by this criterion correspond almost exactly to those specified in Table 3.1. The results of the analysis can thus be legitimately compared with those obtained by Marquand;

(ii)   the industries so derived largely satisfy an alternative criterion of low paying in that they include those industries which were found to have the highest concentrations of low earners. A comparison of Table 3.1 with Tables 2.2 and 2.3 reveals that this association is strongest for manual men. Excepting timber and furniture, the remaining industries in Table 3.1 are those which had the highest concentrations of

manual men earning below £45 (Table 2.2, Column 1). To a
considerable extent, however, this holds true for the other
employment groups examined. For example, clothing and footwear,
the distributive trades and miscellaneous services had high
concentrations of low earners of all employment categories;
(iii) the industries so derived are those where female employment is
most heavily concentrated. In June 1976, the ten industries in
Table 3.1 accounted for 78% of total female employment as
compared with 40% of male employment. (5) Given that women's
earnings are considerably below those of men, the industries
listed are thus likely to include those where average hourly
or weekly earnings, as calculated over all employment
categories, are lowest.

TABLE 3.1   Low Paying Industries
Industries with the Lowest Level of Average Gross
Weekly Earnings for Full-time Manual Men - April 1976

Industry	Average Gross Weekly Earnings (£) *
All industries and services	65.1
All manufacturing industries	67.4
Agriculture, forestry and fishing	51.0
Miscellaneous services	51.0
Clothing and footwear	52.8
Distributive trades	53.9
Public administration and defence	56.8
Professional and scientific services	57.3
Insurance, banking and finance	60.3
Timber, furniture etc.	60.4
Textiles	60.9
Leather, leather goods and fur	na

* Figures relate to those aged 21 and over whose pay was
  unaffected by absence.
Source: NES (1976), op.cit., Part C, Table 54.

2.   CHARACTERISTICS OF LOW PAYING INDUSTRIES

A.   Size of firm

It is often asserted that small firms pay lower wages than larger
firms. Empirical evidence has invariably supported this view and has
shown earnings differentials between firms of differing sizes to be
considerable. The Bolton Report, for example, noted that 'the
difference in earnings between employees in small and large firms is
in the order of 20%'. (6) There are prima facie grounds, therefore,
for supposing that small firms will feature more prominently in low
paying industries than higher paying industries.

The above proposition was tested in relation to manufacturing industries. For each manufacturing Order of SIC 1968, the proportion of the industry's total workforce who worked in establishments of more than 10 but less than 200 employees was calculated. This definition of 'small manufacturing firm' was chosen on the ground that it corresponds closely to that contained in the terms of reference of the Bolton Report. (7) The data related to 1973 and the results are summarised in Table 3.2.

TABLE 3.2   Percentages of Total Employees in Manufacturing Industries Employed in Small Firms - 1973

Industry	% of Employees in small firms (1)
All manufacturing industries	31.9
Timber, furniture etc.	71.3
Clothing and footwear	59.0
Leather, leather goods and fur	54.8 (2)
Metal goods not elsewhere specified	49.6
Paper, printing and publishing	41.8
Bricks, pottery, glass, cement etc.	38.0
Textiles	37.8
Other manufacturing industries	37.0
Mechanical engineering	34.7
Instrument engineering	31.2
Food, drink and tobacco	26.3
Chemicals and allied industries	22.9
Metal manufacture	18.4
Electrical engineering	16.6
Shipbuilding and marine engineering	14.6
Coal and petroleum products	10.9 (2)
Vehicles	10.2

(1) Small firms defined as establishments employing more than 10 but less than 200 employees. Figures refer to total employees in industry (manual, non-manual, full-time, part-time, adults, juveniles, men, women).
(2) Figures relate to firms employing more than 10 and less than 100 employees.
Source: Business Monitor PA 1003, Analysis of UK manufacturing (local) units by employment size (1973), Department of Industry, HMSO, 1976, Table 1.

From the Table it can be seen that the low paying industries were among those with the highest proportions of employees in small firms. 71.3% of total employees in timber and furniture and 59% in clothing and footwear worked in small firms. Nearly 55% of employees in leather worked in firms of less than 100 employees. Textiles ranked seventh with 37% of employees in small firms, a figure well above the all manufacturing industries average. It is also interesting to note that the five industries with the lowest proportions of employees in small firms (metal, electrical engineering, shipbuilding, coal and vehicles) were those recorded in the 1976 NES as having the highest levels of average male manual earnings of all manufacturing industries. The results in the Table correspond closely to a similar test carried out by Marquand.

Outwith the manufacturing sector, statistical information on the relative contribution of small firms to economic activity is scarce. Indeed, for service industries, the Bolton Committee were forced to rely on information relating to 1963 which they collated and estimated from disparate sources. This is reproduced in Table 3.3.

It may be noted from the Table that alternative definitions of 'small firm' were employed in differing industries. For each industry listed, the definition adopted by the Bolton Committee was that which was considered to conform statistically to the three criteria under-lying the Committee's 'economic definition' of small firm. These were: management by owners or part-owners; small market share; and independence, in the sense of not belonging to a larger enterprise. While in the manufacturing sector, firms of less than 200 employees generally satisfied these criteria, firms falling below this employment limit within service industries generally did not, thus necessitating alternative statistical definitions. In all the industries listed, however, 'firms' refer to enterprises rather than establishments.

While somewhat dated, the figures in the Table again suggest the importance of small firms in low paying industries relative to other industry groups. Small firms accounted for 82% of employment and 68% of output in miscellaneous services, 75% of employment and 73% of output in the hotel and catering trades (a sub-category of miscellaneous services in SIC 1968, see Appendix 3.1), and 49% of employment and 32% of output in the retail trades which, in 1976, comprised some 70% of total employment in the distributive trades SIC 1968 Industrial Order. The Table also suggests the importance of small firms in the service sector generally relative to the manufacturing sector where small firms accounted for just 20% of employment and 16% of output. (8)

The remaining low paying industries listed in Table 3.1 (professional and scientific services, insurance, banking and finance and agriculture forestry and fishing) did not fall within the terms of reference of the Bolton Report. The Report did note, however, that 'The majority of enterprises in ... agriculture, the professions and financial services ... are small, in the sense of our terms of reference, and most of our conclusions will apply to them'. (9) In relation to agriculture, specific figures are available from a Report of the NBPI. Of the 116,000 holdings in England and Wales in 1965 which employed one or more regular full-time employees, over 90% employed less than 5 workers. (10)

A further indication of the relative importance of small firms in low paying industries may be obtained from recent evidence relating to wages councils. It is not possible to specify precisely the relative importance of wages councils in the industries listed in Table 3.1, as the coverage of wages board and council orders cuts across SIC industry boundaries. An analysis by Pond and Winyard, however, suggested that the wages council machinery was particularly prominent within the general scope of: agriculture, forestry and fishing (two wages boards); miscellaneous services (six wages councils covering hotels and catering, hairdressing and laundries); the distributive trades (nine wages councils); and clothing and footwear (ten wages councils). (11) An earlier article by Winyard estimated that in the whole of the wages council sector, there were on average only 7 workers per firm (i.e. establishment). For retail distribution the average number of employees per firm was calculated as 4.9 and for hotels and catering the figure was 8.4. (12)

TABLE 3.3   The Relative Importance of Small Firms in Different Industries - 1963

Industry(1)	% of workers employed in small firms	% of net output attributable to small firms(2)	Definition of small firms adopted by Bolton Committee(3)
All industries and services	31	21	Various
Miscellaneous services	82	68	Turnover of £50,000 or less
Hotel and catering trades	75(4)	73(4)	Excluding multiples & brewery managed public houses
Retail trades	49	32	Turnover of £50,000 or less
Road transport	36(4)	26(4)	5 vehicles or less
Building and construction	33	27	25 employees or less
Motor trades	32(4)	29	Turnover of £100,000 or less
Wholesale trades	25	11	Turnover of £200,000 or less
Manufacturing	20	16	200 employees or less
Mining/quarrying	20	20	200 employees or less

(1) Industries listed refer to Industrial Orders and Minimum List Headings of SIC 1958.
(2) Net output = Value of sales minus value of materials purchased (allowing for stock changes).
(3) 'Firms' refer to the 'enterprise' classification.
(4) Estimated figures subject to substantial margin of error.
Source: Bolton Report (1971), op.cit., Table 3.1, p. 33.

Overall, the evidence presented appears to support the proposition
that low paying industries, relative to other industries, are
characterised by large numbers of small firms. There is also support
for the converse proposition, that low paying industries contain
relatively few large firms. On the basis of Census data, it has been
estimated that the shares of the hundred largest enterprises in
employment and output in total manufacturing industry were 37% and
41% respectively in 1968, as compared with 27% and 35% in textiles,
2% and 1% in leather industries, 15% and 10% in clothing and footwear
and 4% and 3% in timber and furniture. (13)

B.   Industrial inefficiency

The link between low pay and industrial inefficiency emerged as a
central and recurring theme in numerous reports issued by the NBPI
throughout the 1960s. The theme was clearly stated in the Fourth
General Report in 1969:

> 'In so far as improving the position of the low paid is one
> of the purposes of a productivity, prices and incomes
> policy - which in our view it should be - the main remedy
> is to be found in the improvement of efficiency. Except in
> a minority of instances therefore, we consider that the
> improvement of the position of the low paid can be subsumed
> in the general problem of improving efficiency'. (14)

A similar, if more guarded viewpoint has been echoed by the TUC on
a number of occasions, where '... at least a partial solution of the
problem of low pay may be in promoting greater efficiency - or by
accelerating the process of putting inefficient companies out of
business'. (15)

Difficulties are encountered in attempting to measure the relative
efficiency of broadly classified groups of industries. No one measure
of efficiency need produce valid comparisons where industries differ
with respect to activities performed, markets or productive processes.
Previous studies have tended, nevertheless, to rely on one of two
measures: a comparison of average rates of return on capital employed
by industry; and a comparison of average net output per employee by
industry. The former ratio is normally estimated from samples of the
financial accounts of companies which have been classified by
industry according to their main activity, the latter from Census of
Production data.

Employing the first approach, Table 3.4 presents estimates of
average return on capital employed by industry for periods between
1960 and 1974. 'Return on capital employed' is defined as the ratio
of net income to net assets. This appears to be the most common definition when comparing broadly classified industries. (16) The data
refer to listed companies and largely exclude the small firm sector.

Data were not available for all the low paying industries listed in
Table 3.1. The figures for those included, however, suggest that
there is no obvious relationship between inefficiency, as indicated
by a low return on capital, and low pay. Indeed the reverse appears
to be the case. In retail distribution, for example, return on

TABLE 3.4 Average Return on Capital Employed - Listed Companies Classified by Industry, 1960-1974

Industry(1)	Net Income as % of Net Assets(2)			
	1960-64	1964-69	1969-73	1973-74
All industries and services(3)	14.02	13.55	15.12	17.60
All manufacturing industries(3)	13.52	13.02	14.32	17.45
Textiles	12.40	13.58	15.24	19.70
Leather, leather goods and fur	11.46	14.43	22.66	22.70
Clothing and footwear	16.12	13.03	14.22	11.80
Timber, furniture etc.	13.54	13.65	23.74	28.15
Wholesale distribution	13.94	14.38	18.00	20.25
Retail distribution	18.94	18.20	21.00	19.80
Miscellaneous services	18.00	14.62	15.02	11.50
Food	15.50	13.58	13.88	16.20
Drink	14.40	13.17	14.94	15.15
Tobacco	15.88	15.00	16.06	14.95
Chemicals and allied industries	12.86	12.60	13.56	20.40
Metal manufacture	11.40	11.02	12.72	17.15
Non-electrical engineering	13.24	12.50	14.32	16.80
Electrical engineering	13.04	14.22	15.76	16.20
Shipbuilding and marine engineering	6.72	2.02	- 3.52	25.15
Vehicles	13.54	12.72	10.06	8.50
Metal goods not elsewhere specified	16.60	15.89	17.16	20.10
Bricks, pottery, glass, cement	17.32	15.12	16.42	18.65
Paper, printing and publishing	13.52	12.32	12.48	17.60
Other manufacturing	13.14	13.47	13.96	14.10
Construction	16.34	16.83	19.08	19.45
Transport and communications	12.48	12.13	14.06	16.65
Companies with mixed activities	-	-	15.00	22.25

(1) Classified by SIC 1968 Orders, except: 'Retail distribution' and 'Wholesale distribution' which together comprise MLH 810-21 of Order XXIII (Distributive trades) of SIC 1968; 'Food', 'Drink' and 'Tobacco' which together comprise Order III (Food, drink and tobacco) of SIC 1968; and 'Non-electrical engineering' which combines Orders VII (Mechanical engineering) and VIII (Instrument engineering) of SIC 1968.

(2) For periods 1960-64 and 1964-69, the data refer to companies with net assets of £0.5 million or more or gross income of £50,000 or more. For periods 1969-73 and 1973-74, the figures relate to companies with net assets of £2.0 million or more or gross income of £200,000 or more.

(3) Companies whose main interests are in agriculture, mining, shipping, insurance, banking and finance, and those operating wholly or mainly abroad, are excluded.

Source: Business Monitor, M3, Company Finance (Seventh Issue), Department of Industry, HMSO, 1976, Table 9.

capital was well above average in all the sub-periods covered, and from 1964, all low paying industries other than clothing and footwear and miscellaneous services experienced above average rates of return. In no period was the average rate of return on capital notably lower for low paying industries than for other industry groups.

Given the relative importance of small firms in low paying industries, these results might be considered unrepresentative. Evidence suggests, however, that the rate of return on capital tends to decrease as company size increases. For example, an inquiry by the Inland Revenue into the accounts of 2,000 companies found that small companies (those with profits of less than £20,000), had a mean rate of return of 14.4%, whereas the rate of return in large quoted companies over the same period (1961-62) was 13.2%. (17) Similar results were obtained in a sample inquiry undertaken by the Bolton Committee, from which it was concluded that 'the suggestion that small companies show a higher rate of return on capital, may be regarded as probably correct. ... the difference in rate of return is not however very great'. (18) It is probable, therefore, that Table 3.4 under-represents rather than overrepresents the relatively higher rates of return in low paying industries.

Turning to the second measure of efficiency commonly employed when dealing with published data, Table 3.5 presents estimates of net output per head, (or average labour productivity), for each manufacturing Order of SIC 1968. The figures relate to 1972, and refer to the total net value of each industry's annual output, as divided by the total number of employees (of all employment categories) in the industry.

The Table shows that productivity was below average in all low paying manufacturing industries. The lowest figure was recorded for clothing and footwear where output per head was only slightly greater than half the all manufacturing industries average. In textiles, the leather industries and timber and furniture, output per head was respectively 77%, 81% and 99% of the all manufacturing industries average. Again, these figures may reflect the relative importance of small firms in low paying industries. On the basis of 1963 Census data the Bolton Committee estimated that average net output per employee in small manufacturing firms was some $23\frac{1}{2}$% below the average for all firms.

Data are not readily available from which output per head in service industries can be estimated and compared. However, low productivity was diagnosed as a chief cause of low pay among manual workers in a number of low paying service industries examined by the NBPI, for example, in local authorities and the NHS. (19) Indeed, it is likely that output per head is substantially lower in low paying service industries than in low paying manufacturing industries, given the overwhelming importance of small firms in a number of these industries (miscellaneous services, catering), and the relative labour intensity of the service sector of the economy.

It would seem, therefore, that when efficiency is measured by return on capital employed, low paying industries are slightly more efficient than other industries, and that when output per head is the yardstick, the opposite is the case. It has been observed that similar results were obtained by the Bolton Committee when measuring the relative efficiency of small and large firms by these same criteria. The

Committee's interpretation of their findings, and conclusions, are thus of interest:

'Neither of these two sets of comparisons indicates anything conclusive about the relative efficiency with which small and large firms use economic resources. This is because the apparently inferior return of small firms in terms of labour employed, is attributable (to an unknown extent) to the smaller amount of capital used per worker, while the apparently superior return on capital by small firms is attributable (again to an unknown extent) to the greater amount of labour employed per unit of capital. What this means is that the proportionate contribution of labour alone to the output of small firms, is greater than the contribution of capital alone, while the reverse is true for large firms. There is no practical way in which the individual contributions of labour and capital to the profit or net output of a firm can be isolated, and therefore no way in which the relative efficiency with which firms use the resources they employ can be compared. All we can conclude is that our analysis so far provides no evidence for assuming that small firms are, in general, any less efficient than large, or vice versa'. (20)

TABLE 3.5 Output Per Head in Manufacturing Industries - 1972

Industry	Output per head (£'s)
All manufacturing industries	2,917
Clothing and footwear	1,573
Textiles	2,240
Shipbuilding and marine engineering	2,259
Instrument engineering	2,321
Leather, leather goods and fur	2,357
Metal goods not elsewhere specified	2,504
Metal manufacture	2,769
Other manufacturing industries	2,771
Electrical engineering	2,781
Vehicles	2,803
Mechanical engineering	2,821
Timber, furniture etc.	2,895
Paper, printing and publishing	3,136
Bricks, pottery, glass, cement	3,232
Food, drink and tobacco	3,734
Chemicals and allied industries	5,054
Coal and petroleum products	7,275

Source: Business Monitor PA 1002, Report on the Census of Production 1972, Summary Tables, Department of Industry, HMSO, 1977, Table 3.

These observations are of equal relevance to the results obtained above. Like small firms, low paying industries are labour intensive with relatively low capital to labour ratios. This applies to the manufacturing sector as well as the service sector, as may be indicated from comparative data on capital expenditure per employee. In 1972, average net capital expenditure per employee for all manufacturing industries was £263, as compared with £190 in textiles, £125 in the leather industries and £54 in clothing and footwear. In retailing, net capital expenditure per employee in 1971 was £125. Furthermore, low paying industries appear to be relatively un-productive and undercapitalised irrespective of the effects of company size. Average output per head in all small manufacturing establishments employing less than 100 employees was £2,524 in 1972, as compared with an average of £2,067 for small establishments in textiles, £2,216 for small establishments in the leather industries and £1,493 for small establishments in clothing and footwear. Average capital expenditure per head in these establishments was £219, whereas in textiles it was £157, in leather, £114 and in clothing and footwear £65. Only in timber and furniture was both productivity and capital expenditure marginally above the all manufacturing industries average for small establishments. (21)

In diagnosing inefficiency as an important cause of low pay among manual workers, the NBPI measured efficiency chiefly in terms of productivity. Low productivity, in turn, was mostly attributed to the poor performance or underutilisation of labour. This was the Board's main conclusion, for example, in their investigation of low pay in local government and the NHS. Given, however, the apparent inter-relation noted above between low productivity and labour intensity, low productivity is not necessarily an adequate indicator of labour inefficiency. It is possible that the Board failed to recognise this point adequately when advocating improvements to labour utilisation as a solution to low pay. Fels, for example, notes that 'The NBPI's early reports contain little recognition of the possibility that low wage low productivity sectors may be exactly the ones in which it is hardest, not easiest, to raise productivity'. (22) He also points out that difficulties in distinguishing the contribution of labour as opposed to that of capital to increases in productivity meant that productivity bargaining throughout the 1960s tended to favour higher paid employees in capital intensive industries, where increases in productivity occurred irrespective of any genuine increases in the contribution or efficiency of labour.

C.   Industrial growth

Low paying industries are often said to be characterised by slow or negative rates of industrial growth. Empirical tests of this proposition have normally been confined to comparisons of rates of growth in employment. In Marquand's analysis, for example, the percentage change in male employment in manufacturing industries was calculated for the period 1960-65. The results led her to conclude 'with confidence' that 'the industries where the lower paid workers are relatively low paid, are mostly industries where employment is contracting'. (23) Similar findings were obtained in a subsequent study undertaken by Bosanquet and Stephens. (24) Here, the analysis focused on the broad difference in earnings levels between manufacturing and service sectors. Again considering only male employees, it was found that for the period 1966-70, employment in manufacturing industry as a whole had increased by 73,000 while employment in two of the largest low paying service industries, miscellaneous services and the distributive trades, had over the same period fallen by approximately 321,000.

Performing a similar analysis, the rates of change in employment in various industries were calculated for periods between 1960 and 1973. Unlike the studies above, however, calculations were made of changes in total employment (both male and female) by industry. The results are summarised in Table 3.6. Included in the Table are all low paying industries, and any other industry that experienced a fall in employment between 1960 and 1973 which was well in excess of average. This latter category includes: mining and quarrying; metal manufacture; and shipbuilding and marine engineering. Employment changes in all industries and services, all production industries and all manufacturing industries have also been calculated to provide comparisons.

The figures show that between 1960 and 1965, (the period corresponding to Marquand's study), employment in the economy as a whole rose by 5.4%. Over the same period, employment in agriculture, forestry and fishing and in all low paying manufacturing industries (excepting timber) substantially declined. Low paying service industries on the other hand grew in employment over this period, and in most cases, the percentage increases in employment in these industries were well in excess of the all industries and services average.

Moving on to the period covered by Bosanquet and Stephen's study, it can be seen that employment in miscellaneous services and distribution did decline between 1965 and 1970. Total employment in all manufacturing industries also declined over this period (-2.9%), though at a lesser rate than in miscellaneous services and distribution. These movements were not, however, typical of the over-all trend. Between 1970 and 1973 employment in manufacturing industries continued to decline at an average rate of -6.1%, while in miscellaneous services and distribution, employment increased by +10.8% and +2.8% respectively.

Viewing the period as a whole, the most significant changes in employment which have occurred in low paying industries have been a large loss of labour from agriculture and the low paying manufacturing industries, matched by a considerable expansion of employment in low paying service industries. Throughout the first half of the 1960s, the decline in low paying manufacturing industries took place against a slight overall growth in the manufacturing sector. Thereafter, the manufacturing sector as a whole began to decline.

Of the other industries, which experienced particularly high losses of labour over this period, the decline in mining and quarrying possibly reflects the large scale redundancies which occurred in coal mining as a result of pit closures. Similarly, the introduction of rationalisation and capital restructuring schemes in metal manufacture, (particularly British Steel), and in shipbuilding possibly accounts for the large shakeout of labour from these industries throughout the 1960s and early 1970s.

TABLE 3.6   Trends in Employment - Selected Industries, 1960-73

Industry	Percentage change in employment			
	1960-65	1966-70	1970-73	1960-73
All industries and services	+ 5.4	+ 3.5	+ 0.9	+ 3.4
Production industries *	+ 2.1	- 6.8	- 5.4	- 9.9
Manufacturing industries *	+ 1.8	- 2.9	- 6.1	- 7.0
Agriculture, forestry & fishing	-18.4	-19.6	- 7.2	-41.6
Textiles	- 8.8	-10.4	-12.3	-29.3
Leather, leather goods and fur	- 3.5	-11.1	- 8.3	-22.8
Clothing and footwear	- 6.3	-11.0	- 2.8	-20.1
Timber, furniture etc.	+ 2.5	- 6.3	+ 8.3	+ 2.1
Distributive trades	+ 6.4	- 8.4	+ 2.8	+ 0.6
Insurance, banking and finance	+21.8	+16.7	+10.6	+60.4
Professional & scientific services	+21.4	+11.6	+12.0	+58.6
Miscellaneous services	+14.3	- 6.1	+10.8	+20.3
Public administration & defence	+ 6.7	+ 4.0	+ 6.7	+22.7
Mining and quarrying	-19.0	-28.1	-11.3	-52.4
Metal manufacture	+ 2.2	- 5.4	-13.0	-17.3
Shipbuilding & marine engineering	-19.0	- 8.1	- 2.2	-28.6

* Manufacturing industries comprise SIC Orders III to XIX.
Production industries comprise Orders II to XXI, that is, all manufacturing industries plus mining and quarrying, construction and gas, electricity and water.
Source: Department of Employment Gazette, March 1975, Table 5, pp. 197-202.

Trends in employment in low paying industries appear to represent a sharper example of a more general and gradual change which seems to have taken place in the industrial employment structure in Great Britain, that is, the decline in employment in the industry or productive sectors of the economy, concomitant with large increases in service sector employment. These movements are a continuation of pre-war trends but appear to have gained impetus in the early 1960s and increased in momentum into the 1970s. The extent of the change is calculated in Table 3.7.

The Table shows that the share of production industries in total employment fell from 50.2% in 1960 to 43.7% in 1973. The service sector on the other hand increased its share of total employment from 46.5% in 1960 to 54.4% in 1973. The share of agriculture also declined considerably, accounting for just 1.9% of total employment in 1973. These changes reflect only in part, a movement of employment from production to service industries. They also reflect increases in employment in the economy generally over this period, particularly increases in female employment. Between 1960 and 1973 women's employment increased by 1,287,000 (+17.3%) while male employment fell over the same period by some 553,000 (-3.9%). Most of these women appear to have been attracted to service industries where female employment increased by some 1.5 million. (25) Hence some part of the relative increase in the share of service industries in total employment will reflect new entrants into the labour market rather than transfers of employment from production industries.

TABLE 3.7   Changes in the Shares of Industry, Services and Agriculture in Total Employment, 1960-73

Employment sector *	Share of total employment (%)	
	1960	1973
Production industries	50.2	43.7
Manufacturing industries	38.4	34.6
Service industries	46.5	54.4
Agriculture, forestry and fishing	3.4	1.9

* Production industries and manufacturing industries are as defined in Table 3.6. Service industries comprise Orders XXII to XXVII of SIC 1968, that is, all low paying service industries in addition to transport and communication.

Source: Department of Employment Gazette, March 1975, op.cit.,

Turning to other indicators of industrial growth, Table 3.8 presents estimates of percentage changes in output and productivity in selected industries for various periods between 1960 and 1973. Apart from minor differences in the groupings of industrial categories, the industries included in the Table are largely the same as those included in Table 3.6. Some insight can thus be obtained of the interrelation of movements in employment, productivity and output.

It can be seen from the Table that declining employment in agriculture and the low paying manufacturing industries has generally been accompanied by considerable gains in productivity between 1960 and 1973. Excepting leather, the rates of growth of productivity in these industries were generally above the all industries and services average. Again excepting leather, these industries also grew in output throughout this period though in most cases the growth in output (excepting timber) was slightly below the all industries and services average.

For low paying service industries, a differing pattern emerges. Like low paying manufacturing industries, these industries grew in output between 1960 and 1973. Growth rates were comparable with (or marginally above) the all industries and services average. Excepting distribution, however, the growth in productivity in service industries was well below average. For a large part of the service sector, expanding employment was accompanied by an actual decline in productivity between 1971 and 1973.

Of the other industries contained in the Table, the large loss of labour in mining and quarrying, metal manufacture and shipbuilding

TABLE 3.8   Trends in Productivity and Output - Selected
             Industries, 1960-73

| Industry | Percentage changes per annum | | | | | |
| | Output | | | Output per head | | |
	1960-65	1966-71	1971-73	1960-65	1966-71	1971-73
All industries and services	+3.1	+2.2	+ 4.1	+2.0	+ 3.4	+2.8
Manufacturing industries	+3.2	+2.2	+ 5.2	+2.8	+ 3.6	+6.7
Agriculture, forestry and fishing	+2.9	+3.1	+ 2.3	+6.2	+10.1	+2.3
Textiles	+1.7	+3.2	+ 3.6	+4.0	+ 7.7	+6.0
Leather, leather goods and fur	+0.9	-0.9	- 1.0	+1.7	+ 2.3	+1.8
Clothing & footwear	+0.9	+0.9	+ 3.9	+2.4	+ 3.6	+5.3
Timber, furniture etc.	+4.5	+1.4	+12.4	+3.9	+ 2.7	+8.0
Distributive trades	+2.6	+1.4	+ 5.8	+1.4	+ 3.9	+3.1
Other services *	+3.5	+3.1	+ 4.4	+0.4	+ 1.9	-0.2
Mining and quarrying	-0.5	-2.9	- 3.1	+3.6	+ 4.5	+1.2
Metal manufacture	+2.0	-1.3	+ 4.3	+1.5	+ 1.0	+8.2
Engineering and shipbuilding **	+4.1	+3.4	+ 4.9	+2.5	+ 4.3	+7.3

* Includes: insurance, banking and finance; professional and
   scientific services; and miscellaneous services.
** Includes: mechanical engineering; electrical engineering; and
   shipbuilding and marine engineering.
Source: National Institute Economic Review, No. 71, National
        Institute of Economic and Social Research, February 1975,
        p. 18.

appears again to have been associated with large gains in
productivity. Rates of growth in productivity in these industries
were comparable with, and for some years, greater than the average
rate for all industries and services. The percentage increase in
mining and quarrying between 1971 and 1973 (+1.2%) is not a
representative figure as it reflects loss of production owing to
industrial unrest in 1972. From the same source, the growth in
productivity in mining and quarrying between 1971 and 1972 was
-12.1%, while the growth from 1972 to 1973 was +16.5%. The growth in
output in these industries varied. In engineering and shipbuilding,
growth in output was above average in each sub-period. In metal
manufacture, growth rates were comparable in some periods though
negative growth occurred between 1966-71. Mining and quarrying
experienced negative growth rates in all three sub-periods.
    Summing up, the results obtained suggest that no simple relation-
ship exists between low pay and industrial growth. The relation is
found to vary according to each indicator of growth considered. An

important general finding, however, is that recent patterns of growth
in agriculture and low paying manufacturing industries generally
differ from, and indeed are largely opposite to, those characterising
low paying service industries.

D.   Sex composition

It has previously been noted that the employment of women is largely
confined to low paying industries. A further suggestion often made is
that the ratio of women to men is relatively high in industries where
earnings of men are relatively low. This proposition found only
limited support in Marquand's analysis, where the association was
found to exist only in the textile and clothing industries. In testing
the proposition in relation to more recent data, and extending the
test to low paying service industries, a more positive association was
found. The results are summarised in Table 3.9. The Table shows that
with the exceptions of public administration, agriculture and timber,
the proportions of women in remaining low paying industries were
above the all industries and services average.

TABLE 3.9   Women's Employment as a Proportion of Total Employment –
Selected Industries, June 1976

Industry	Total employees (thousands)	% women
All industries and services	22539	41
Manufacturing industries	7246	29
Clothing and footwear	381	76
Professional & scientific services	3655	68
Miscellaneous services	2299	58
Distributive trades	2723	55
Insurance, banking and finance	1103	51
Textiles	513	45
Leather, leather goods and fur	40	44
Public administration and defence	1627	37
Agriculture, forestry and fishing	395	25
Timber, furniture etc.	264	19

Source: Department of Employment Gazette, December 1977, pp. 1355-57.

E.   Skill composition

It has been observed that the only characteristic which appeared to be
shared by the low paying industries examined by the NBPI was a low
general level of employee skill. The extent to which this applies to
low paying industries generally is now considered.

Data on the skill levels of employees by industry are scarce.
However, between 1964 and 1968, the Ministry of Labour published a
series in which all occupations in manufacturing industries were

assigned to one of four broad occupational categories. These were: 'administrative, technical and clerical'; 'skilled operatives'; 'mainly semi-skilled'; and 'others'. After 1968, the series was discontinued. Table 3.10 outlines the proportions of total employees in manufacturing industries generally, and in low paying manufacturing industries, who were allocated to each category in 1968.

TABLE 3.10   Classification of Total Employment by Broad Skill Category - Selected Manufacturing Industries, May 1968

Industry (2)	Proportions in each category(%)(1)			
	Admin. technical & clerical (3)	Skilled operatives (4)	Mainly semi- skilled (5)	Others (6)
All manufacturing industries	26.2	31.9	21.2	20.2
Textiles	14.8	29.6	35.4	20.1
Leather, leather goods & fur	18.1	42.9	18.7	20.4
Clothing	13.5	62.1	13.6	10.8
Footwear	14.5	58.3	17.3	9.9
Timber, furniture etc.	20.7	48.7	6.1	24.6

(1) Percentages may not sum to 100 because of rounding.
(2) Classified according to SIC 1958. For the industries listed, however, SIC 1958 and SIC 1968 are identical, except for clothing and footwear industries which are classified within a single Order in SIC 1968.
(3) All non-manual staff.
(4) Employees who have undergone a period of apprenticeship, or a minimum of 6 month's training or whose jobs require considerable experience to attain proficiency.
(5) Employees in jobs which require at least one month's training or experience to attain proficiency.
(6) Unskilled employees in jobs for which no training and little experience are required to attain proficiency.
Source: British Labour Statistics - Historical Abstract, 1886-1968, Department of Employment, HMSO, 1971, Table 149.

The Table shows that among manual employees, the three skill categories were distinguished according to one criterion - required length of training or experience to achieve proficiency. Whether this is an adequate indicator of skill is a matter of some debate. The criterion by which manual occupations were distinguished from non-manual was not, however, revealed. Given, however that occupations included under the non-manual category included such as 'routine clerk', 'receptionist' and 'cashier', it is unclear what proportion of jobs in the 'administrative, technical and clerical' category were of higher general skill content, in terms of required qualifications, training or experience, than those assigned manual status.

Bearing these considerations in mind, the figures in the Table provide little support for the proposition that low paying industries contain relatively high proportions of unskilled manual labour. The proportions of employees in low paying industries categorised under 'others', the least skilled group, were, with the exception of timber and furniture, approximately equal to, or lower than the average proportion for all manufacturing industries. Similarly, excepting textiles, the proportions of employees in the semi-skilled bracket were below average in low paying industries. Again excepting textiles, low paying industries appeared on the other hand to contain above average proportions of skilled operatives. Only in textiles, therefore, where the proportions of unskilled and semi-skilled combined were above average, could the skill levels of manual workers be considered relatively low. The proportions of workers employed in non-manual occupations were, however, much lower in low paying industries than in manufacturing industry generally.

These findings largely coincide with Marquand's. Again employing the Ministry of Labour classification of skill, it was found that there was no tendency for manufacturing industries with low earnings for manual men, to be industries which employed relatively high proportions of unskilled men. Indeed, there was a slight tendency for industries with a high proportion of unskilled men to have slightly higher earnings relative to other industries. In attempting to explain these results, Marquand suggested that unskilled workers may be organised more strongly than skilled workers. Elsewhere, however, it has been suggested that skilled employees tend on the whole to be better organised than the unskilled. (26) An alternative explanation may relate to the employment trends noted previously. Low paying manufacturing industries have been declining in employment since 1960 and probably before. (27) The higher proportions of skilled employees in these industries may simply reflect a lower priority accorded to the unskilled in times of redundancies. Routh has demonstrated that alterations in the proportion of unskilled manual workers in an industry are associated with changes in the employment size of the industry, whereas the proportion of skilled manual workers tends to be unaffected by industry growth or decline. (28)

Except for the retail trades, there does not appear to be a corresponding classification of service sector jobs into broad skill bands. For retailing, the information again relates to 1968 and is limited to workers employed in large shops, that is, in shops employing more than 100 workers. Seven broad occupational categories were distinguished: 'administrative and office'; 'specialist staff'; 'skilled maintenance staff'; 'employees undergoing training'; 'sales supervisors, section heads and first assistants'; 'other sales staff'; and 'other staff'. The proportions of males, females and total employees who fell within each of these categories are calculated in Table 3.11.

These categories do not necessarily imply differences in the skill content of jobs. It may be assumed, however, that the two categories of least skill in terms of required training or experience are 'other sales staff' and 'other staff'. The former consists of general sales staff with no supervisory role or authority, and as such, it is likely that these employees would require little more than a month's training or experience to achieve job proficiency. Hence, it would not seem unreasonable to assign, at most, semi-skilled status to this category. The examples of jobs classified under 'other staff' (restaurant staff, van attendants, labourers et al), suggest, on the other hand, that employees so categorised would come closer to the definition of unskilled, as employed for manufacturing industries.

TABLE 3.11   Occupational Breakdown of Employees in Large Shops (1) - May 1968

Occupational category	Proportion in each category (%)		
	Males	Females Full-time Part-time	Total
Administrative and office	18.1	20.1	7.3	15.9
Specialist staff (2)	9.2	7.2	2.5	6.3
Skilled maintenance staff (3)	4.2	–	–	1.1
Employees undergoing training	0.7	0.2	–	0.3
Sales supervisors, section heads and first assistants	7.1	7.7	0.2	5.4
Other sales staff	32.5	52.1	73.5	53.4
Other staff (4)	28.2	12.6	16.5	17.7
All categories (5)	100.0	100.0	100.0	100.0

(1) Defined as shops employing more than 100 employees.
(2) Window dressers, hair stylists, manicurists et al.
(3) Employees who have undergone a period of apprenticeship or have had equivalent training.
(4) Restaurant staff, van attendants, warehouse workers, labourers et al.
(5) Percentages may not sum to 100 because of rounding.
Source: Employment and Productivity Gazette, December 1968, Table 3, p. 999.

If these assumptions are realistic, the figures in the Table suggest that large shops employ very high proportions of unskilled and semi-skilled labour. Over 70% of total employees fell within the categories 'other sales staff' and 'other staff'. 90% of part-time women, over 64% of full-time women and over 60% of men fell within these categories. It is probable that the proportions of employees in large shops who may be viewed in any meaningful sense as skilled (e.g. specialist staff, skilled maintenance, managers, accountants), is considerably higher than in the retail trades generally. As was shown in Table 3.3, almost half of all employees in retailing are employed in small enterprises, (as defined by sales turnover), which are less likely to employ specialist staff or provide training facilities.

In the absence of specific data, some indication of skill levels in remaining low paying service industries may be obtained by examining the age structure of service sector employees. From unpublished NES data relating to 1970, Bosanquet and Stephens noted that unskilled male workers tended to be older employees. In 1970, 39% of unskilled male manual workers were aged over 50 as against 33% of all male manual workers. However, in public administration and defence, 50% of male manual workers were over 50, in professional and scientific services, the figure was 46% and in insurance, banking and finance, 45% of male manual workers were aged over 50. 78% of male cleaners and charmen were aged over 50 in 1970. (29)

More recent, published, NES data do not classify employee age by industry, but only by occupation. Nevertheless, a number of CODOT occupational groupings are readily identifiable with SIC Industrial Orders. For example, the group X category, 'Catering, cleaning, hairdressing and other personal services', consists of occupations mainly associated with miscellaneous services. In 1976, 44% of male employees in group X occupations were aged over 50 as compared with an all occupations average of 28%. Similarly, 31% of male employees in group XI occupations 'Farming, fishing and related' were aged over 50. (30)

It has been noted that the employment of women is particularly concentrated in low paying service industries. In 1976, women's employment in the economy as a whole, expressed as a percentage of total employment was 41%. In the five low paying service industries, on the other hand, women comprised over 58% of total employment. 73% of all women in employment were employed in these five industries as compared with 37% of men. (31) A comparison of the job and educational qualifications of women and men may thus further indicate the relative skill content of service occupations in terms of job complexity, educational or training requirements.

Educational and job qualifications appear to differ markedly between the sexes, as the following statistics indicate. In 1971, male students at British universities outnumbered female students by a ratio of 12 to 5. In the age group 25-34 only 2% of women as compared with $7\frac{1}{2}$% of men held a university degree. Of workers in employment, nearly half a million men as compared with 100,000 women attended grant-aided day-release establishments in 1971. In the same year 39% of boys as compared with 8% of girls entered apprenticeships. 54% of women between the ages of 15-24, 59% between the ages of 25-34 and 90% aged 65 and over possessed no educational qualifications whatsoever in 1971 as compared with 48%, 48% and 80% respectively for men. (32) Or again, in 1975 in Britain, 76% of women in employment as compared with 53% of men had received less than one month's training. On the other hand, 29% of men as compared with 8% of women had received four year's or more training, and 12% of men as compared with 6% of women over a year's training. (33)

It is all the more surprising in this context that low paying manufacturing industries were generally found to contain above average proportions of skilled employees, given that these industries also contain relatively high proportions of women. The skill levels of women in these industries appear, however, to be on a par with, if not above, those of men. In 1968, 66% of all women employed in clothing fell within the category 'skilled operative' as against 48% of men. Similarly, 61% of women in footwear were classified as skilled as against 56% of men. In textiles and the leather industries the proportions of skilled women were only marginally below those of men. Only in timber was a significantly higher proportion of men than women classified as skilled. (34) It is almost certain, however, that low paying manufacturing industries are unusual in this respect. One unusual feature of women's employment in these industries is that comparatively few are employed on a part-time basis. In 1976, 34% of all women employed were part-timers as compared with 24% of women in textiles, 23% of women in clothing and footwear and 24% of women in the leather industries. In low paying service industries on the other hand, 40% of women in the distributive trades, 49% in miscellaneous services and 42% in professional and scientific services were employed on a part-time basis. (35)

As regards agriculture, some indication of the skill levels of employees may be obtained from the work of the NBPI. In June 1966, by far the largest number of regular employees in agriculture in England and Wales, (comprising some 45% of total regular employment), fell within the category 'general farmworker', a title implying little in the way of special ability, training or experience. While some of the titles of the remaining occupational categories into which employees were classified implied a greater degree of specialisation and skill ('bailiffs and foremen', 'dairy cowmen', 'stockmen', 'tractor men', 'market gardeners', 'others'), each of these accounted for less than 10% of total regular employment. On the other hand, some 44% of total employment in agriculture was made up of casual or seasonal workers in June 1966, an employment group denoting little in the way of skill by whatever criteria measured. (36)

In conclusion, it would seem that low paying industries differ with respect to the general skill levels possessed by workers or demanded by occupations. Once again, the manufacturing/services distinction appears to be of importance. As measured by contemporary criteria, low paying manufacturing industries do not appear to contain relatively high proportions of unskilled manual labour. However, the weight of evidence does suggest a low general level of employee skill in agriculture and low paying service industries.

F. Trade Union density

It has been noted that wage rates in many low paying industries are largely determined by recourse to the wages council machinery, thereby indicating ineffective collective bargaining arrangements or a low level of trade union membership. A more precise measure of the relative strength of trade union organisation in low paying industries may be obtained by comparing trade union density levels by industry. The level of trade union density in an industry refers to the proportion of an industry's total workforce (employed and unemployed) who belong to a trade union.

Table 3.12 provides figures for union density in the economy generally in 1974, in the manufacturing sector, and for each low paying industry respectively. The data derive from a study undertaken by Price and Bain of movements in union density between 1948 and 1974. (37) The authors made use of unpublished Department of Employment data and, in order to provide valid comparisons for the period examined, the 1974 data were classified according to SIC 1948. In Table 3.12, however, the figures have been rearranged as far as possible into SIC 1968 industry groupings.

TABLE 3.12   Trade Union Density by Industry - Selected
              Industries, 1974

Industry (1)	Trade Union density (%)(2)
All industries and services	50.4
All manufacturing industries	62.2
Public administration and defence (including educational services)	86.5
Clothing and footwear	63.9
Leather, leather goods and fur	46.6
Professional and scientific services (excluding educational services)	44.6
Insurance, banking and finance (3)	44.2
Textiles	40.9
Timber, furniture etc.	35.2
Agriculture, forestry and fishing	23.3
Miscellaneous services (4)	16.3
Distributive trades	11.4

(1) Apart from the inclusion of education within public administration
    and defence, industry groupings correspond to SIC 1968 Orders.
(2) Trade union density refers to total union membership in industry
    expressed as a % of total employed (and unemployed) in industry.
(3) Excludes MLH headings 863-866 (see Appendix 3.1). Industries
    covered accounted for 61% of total employment in this Order in
    June 1974.
(4) Includes hotels and catering, entertainment and media services and
    sport and other recreations which together accounted for 47% of
    employment in this Order in June 1974. Excludes MLH headings 883,
    889-899 (see Appendix 3.1).
Source: R. Price and G.S. Bain, Union Growth Revisited: 1948-1974 in
        Perspective, British Journal of Industrial Relations, November
        1976, Table 3, pp. 342-43. The authors' figures were adjusted
        to the SIC 1968 classification through reference to manpower
        data contained in Department of Employment Gazette, July 1974,
        pp. 632-35, and Department of Employment Gazette, July 1975,
        pp. 647-49.

It can be seen from the Table that for all low paying industries
other than public administration and defence and clothing and footwear,
trade union density levels were below the all industries and services
aggregate level. Union density was particularly low in agriculture
(23.3%), miscellaneous services (16.3%) (38) and the distributive
trades (11.4%). Union density in the manufacturing sector as a whole
was above that for the economy generally. However, in all low paying
manufacturing industries other than clothing and footwear, union
density was well below the average manufacturing sector level. With
one or two exceptions, therefore, it may be concluded that trade union
density levels in low paying industries are generally below average.

G.   Industrial payments structures

The incidence of low earnings is sometimes linked to certain features of the payments structures of low paying industries. Evidence gathered by Fisher and Dix, for example, suggested that the earnings of male manual employees in low paying industries were tied relatively closely to basic pay, so that there was a lesser opportunity to enhance basic earnings through some combination of overtime, bonus or shift premium payments. (39) Marquand, on the other hand, found that earnings in some low paying industries were tied relatively closely to nationally negotiated wage rates. The extent to which these two features characterise the payments structures of low paying industries generally was examined.

Details of the make-up of average gross weekly earnings by industry are available from the NES. The survey distinguishes four components of earnings: overtime pay; payment by results (PBR) payments; shift premium payments; and all other pay. This latter category includes not only basic pay, but any additional items of pay not covered by the other three categories, such as service pay, London weighting and special duties payments. However, since these additional items normally constitute a very small proportion of total earnings, the all other pay factor is often employed as a close approximation of basic pay.

NES data show that it is among full-time manual men that the greatest gap occurs between basic pay, as indicated by the all other pay factor, and total earnings. In 1976, the all other pay component, expressed as a percentage of total average gross weekly earnings, was 75.4% for manual men, 94.5% for non-manual men, 86.1% for manual women and 97.9% for non-manual women. Overtime and PBR payments were particularly important components of male manual earnings, accounting for 13.4% and 8.0% respectively of total average gross weekly earnings. Shift premium payments accounted for a further 3.2% of earnings. For manual women, overtime and shift premium payments were of minor importance and accounted for just 2.5% and 1.9% respectively of total earnings, though PBR schemes made an important contribution to pay, accounting for 9.4% of total average gross weekly earnings in 1976. (40)

Focusing on full-time manual men, Table 3.13 presents data on the make-up of average gross weekly earnings of manual men in all industries and services, in all manufacturing industries and in each low paying industry respectively. The four components of earnings are expressed in the Table as percentages of total average earnings, so that their relative importance can be compared among the industries listed. The figures in the all other pay column thus give some indication of the extent to which earnings in low paying industries are tied relatively closely to basic pay.

It can be seen from the Table that the all other pay factor constituted a relatively high proportion of total earnings only in agriculture and low paying service industries (excluding public administration). In the remaining industries, the joint contribution of overtime, PBR and shift premium payments was roughly equal to, and in the case of textiles, above the all industries and services average. This difference mainly reflects the differing contribution of PBR payments to total earnings in each group of industries. In public administration and defence and the low paying manufacturing industries, PBR payments appear to be a particularly important component of earnings, especially in clothing and footwear and timber, while in agriculture and low paying service industries, PBR payments contributed relatively little to total earnings. With respect to over-time and shift premium payments, however, low paying manufacturing and service industries were broadly similar. In general, these components made a lesser than average contribution to total earnings in low paying industries. Overtime payments were nevertheless an important component of earnings, and with the exceptions of clothing and footwear and miscellaneous services, the contribution of overtime to total earnings in low paying industries did not differ markedly from average.

TABLE 3.13   Make-up of Average Gross Weekly Earnings of Full-time Manual Men (1), Selected Industries, 1976

Industry	Components as percentages of total(2)			
	Overtime pay	PBR etc. payments	Shift etc. premium payments	All(3) other pay
All industries and services	13.4	8.0	3.2	75.4
All manufacturing industries	13.3	9.0	4.0	73.8
Textiles	12.5	10.2	4.6	72.8
Clothing and footwear	5.9	18.4	0.2	75.4
Timber, furniture etc.	10.0	13.7	0.3	76.0
Public administration and defence	10.2	11.4	1.4	76.9
Professional and scientific services	12.1	4.1	3.8	80.0
Distributive trades	12.2	4.9	1.5	81.4
Agriculture, forestry and fishing	11.1	5.9	0.2	82.7
Insurance, banking and finance	12.6	3.0	1.1	83.3
Miscellaneous services	9.5	4.6	0.9	85.1

(1) Figures relate to men aged 21 and over whose pay was unaffected by absence.
(2) Percentages may not sum to 100 because of rounding.
(3) Includes not only basic pay but any other item other than overtime payments, PBR etc. payments and shift etc. premium payments.
Source: NES (1976), op.cit., Part C, Table 79.

The relation of basic pay to total earnings for the remaining employment categories in low paying industries was broadly similar to that in other industries. For non-manual men, manual and non-manual women, basic pay generally accounted for well over 90% of total average earnings in all industries. Two interesting exceptions, however, were for manual women in textiles and clothing and footwear. In these industries, the all other pay component, expressed as a percentage of total average earnings, was 71.3% in textiles and 70.6% in clothing and footwear, as against an all industries and services figure of 86.1%. Again, the main component of earnings, other than basic pay, was PBR payments which accounted for 26.1% of total earnings in textiles and 28.3% in clothing and footwear as compared with 9.4% in all industries and services. (41)

In sum, the evidence indicates that for manual men, earnings are tied relatively closely to basic pay in agriculture and low paying service industries (excluding public administration), but not in low paying manufacturing industries. For manual women in low paying manufacturing industries, basic pay is a smaller than average component of earnings. These results appear to reflect the differing opportunities afforded to employees in each group of industries to enhance basic pay through systems of payment by results.

Information relating to the gap between industrial earnings and nationally negotiated wage rates is less systematic. Data on average or standard wage rates or minima are rarely classified by industry owing to the difficulties of fitting information on collective agreements and wages council orders into SIC Industrial Orders. In Marquand's analysis, national and local government services were cited as examples of low paying industries where earnings were tied relatively closely to wage rates, though no comparative statistical evidence was produced to support this contention.

The data contained in Table 3.13 can perhaps be taken as some evidence of the relative proximity of earnings to national wage rates, at least in low paying service industries where PBR payments (which are often determined locally rather than nationally) constitute a relatively small component of earnings. This, however, is an insufficient indicator. National and local rates can differ with respect to a number of components of earnings, including basic pay. Data from the NES 1968 show, for example, that for all men in the survey (manual and non-manual) for whom a nationally negotiated basic rate was applicable, actual basic pay was, on average, some $6\frac{1}{2}\%$ higher than the nationally negotiated rate. (42)

Perhaps the best indicator of the relative proximity of earnings to rates can be obtained by comparing the industrial incidence of 'wage drift'. Wage drift is the term used to describe changes in the gap between earnings and rates over time. Hence, an industrial comparison of the incidence of wage drift may both indicate and in some part account for differences in the proximity of earnings to rates in different industries.

There are many approaches to measuring wage drift. In published data, however, drift is most commonly calculated by deducting annual percentage changes in average hourly wage rates for male manual workers from annual percentage changes in their average hourly wage earnings. Overtime payments are usually excluded from the calculation of average hourly earnings, since overtime rates are mainly determined nationally and payments rarely exceed national rates, though shift premium payments (where this is also the case) and PBR payments are usually included in statistical measurements.

Comparative data on wage drift by industry are again scarce, owing to the classification difficulties noted above. On the basis of unpublished Department of Employment data, however, the Office of Manpower Economics produced comparative estimates of drift in thirteen industries, mainly in the manufacturing sector, for the period 1961 to 1971. Included among these were the four low paying manufacturing industries. Drift was calculated as above, by estimating the difference between annual percentage changes in average hourly wage earnings (excluding overtime) and average hourly wage rates for full-time manual men. The results are summarised in Table 3.14.

TABLE 3.14   Wage Drift in Selected Industries, 1961-1971

Industry	Wage drift (1)
All industries and services	+1.5
Food, drink and tobacco	+2.1
Clothing and footwear	+1.9
All metals (2)	+1.8
Gas, electricity and water	+1.8
Paper, printing and publishing	+1.5
Transport and communications	+1.4
Construction	+1.2
Other manufacturing industries	+1.1
Bricks, pottery, glass, cement etc.	+0.8
Timber and furniture etc.	+0.8
Leather, leather goods and fur	+0.8
Textiles	+0.7
Chemicals and allied industries (3)	+0.1

(1) Wage drift defined as: average annual percentage rate of growth in average hourly earnings (excluding overtime), 1961-1971 - minus - average annual percentage rate of growth in average hourly wage rates, 1961-1971. Figures refer to the pay of full-time manual men aged 21 and over whose pay was unaffected by absence.
(2) Comprises Orders V to IX in SIC 1958; and Orders VI and XII in SIC 1968 (i.e. all types of engineering and shipbuilding and the manufacture of vehicles, metal and metal goods.
(3) Comprises Order IV in SIC 1958; and Orders IV and V in SIC 1968.
Source: Wage Drift: Review of Literature and Research, Office of Manpower Economics, HMSO, 1973, Table 3, Annexe to Chapter 2, and Table 2, Annexe to Chapter 5.

From the Table, it can be seen that the incidence of drift in timber and furniture, the leather industries and textiles was substantially below average. Only in chemicals was there a lower incidence of drift. Drift in clothing and footwear, on the other hand, was well above average, possibly reflecting the very high contribution which PBR payments make to total earnings in this industry.

Some additional evidence on drift is contained in the Donovan

Commission's Report. The Commission classified a number of SIC 1958 Industrial Orders into four groups according to the relationship which was thought to exist in each Industrial Order between nationally determined rates and actual levels of pay. In this classification, actual earnings included the effects of overtime. (43) Included in the category where rates were thought to be closest to earnings were: education services (a sub-category of professional and scientific services in SIC 1968); local and national government services (i.e. public administration and defence in SIC 1968); agriculture; and clothing. The inclusion of clothing in this category possibly reflects the low incidence of overtime in this industry. Alternatively, the reason could be that an appreciable gap between earnings and rates occurs only in footwear. Textiles was classified with those industries where only a minority of employees were thought to earn well in excess of nationally determined rates. Distribution, on the other hand, was included in the category of industries where the actual pay of the majority of employees was thought to be well in excess of rates. It is to be remembered, however, that the few centrally determined rates which apply in distribution are largely those as specified in Wages Council Regulations, and as such, are normally set at very low levels. No information existed on the relation of earnings to rates in remaining low paying industries. (44)

Overall, the weight of evidence suggests that with the possible exception of clothing and footwear and distribution, the earnings of manual men in low paying industries are tied relatively closely to nationally negotiated wage rates, or at least tend to diverge to a lesser extent from these rates over time.

3. SUMMARY AND CONCLUSIONS

1. General Broadly classified groups of low paying industries share many characteristics in common and generally differ from other industries with respect to these. Low paying industries are, however, dissimilar in a number of important respects. In particular, the manufacturing/service distinction appears to be of importance when considering the characteristics of low paying industries.

2. Size of firm Low paying industries, relative to other industries, are characterised by large numbers of small firms. Support was also found for the converse proposition, that low paying industries contain relatively few large firms.

3. Inefficiency The results obtained provide no grounds for assuming that low paying industries are, in general, any less (or more) efficient than other industries. Measured in terms of return on capital employed, low paying industries appear to be slightly more efficient than other industries, while they are relatively less efficient when output per head or average labour productivity is employed as the measure of efficiency. However, low paying industries were found to be labour intensive, and since both measures of efficiency are themselves influenced by differing capital/labour ratios, neither measure produces valid inter-industry comparisons. In particular, it is unknown to what

extent low productivity in low paying industries simply reflects labour intensity as opposed to labour inefficiency.

4. <u>Industrial growth</u> Agriculture and low paying manufacturing industries differ from low paying service industries with respect to recent trends in employment, productivity and output. Over the periods examined, agriculture and low paying manufacturing industries generally experienced above average losses of labour, rates of growth in productivity which were close to or above average and rates of growth in output marginally below the average rate. Low paying service industries over the same periods generally experienced above average growth in employment, below average or negative growth in productivity and rates of growth in output which were marginally above the average rate. Trends in employment in low paying industries appear to be related to a more general and gradual pattern of post-war change in the industrial employment structure in Great Britain.

5. <u>Sex composition</u> Low paying industries generally contain relatively high proportions of female employees.

6. <u>Skill composition</u> No support was found for the proposition that low paying manufacturing industries contain relatively high proportions of unskilled manual employees. On the contrary, the skill levels of manual employees in these industries were generally found to be above average. However, the ratio of manual to non-manual employees appears to be relatively high in these industries. Agriculture and low paying service industries, on the other hand, do appear to contain relatively high proportions of unskilled workers, particularly women.

7. <u>Union density</u> Trade union density is generally below average in low paying industries.

8. <u>Industrial payments structures</u> Total earnings of manual men tend to be tied relatively closely to basic pay in agriculture and low paying service industries, but not in low paying manufacturing industries. In the latter, PBR payments constitute a higher than average proportion of total male manual earnings, while the reverse is generally the case in agriculture and low paying service industries. In most low paying industries, however, the earnings of manual men are tied relatively closely to nationally determined wage rates, or at least tend to diverge to a lesser extent from these rates over time.

APPENDIX 3.1   Low Paying Industries by Industrial Order and
                Minimum List Heading - Standard Industrial
                Classification, 1968

Minimum List Heading *   Order I - Agriculture, Forestry and Fishing

        001   Agriculture and horticulture
        002   Forestry
        003   Fishing

                          Order XII - Textiles

        411   Production of man-made fibres
        412   Spinning and doubling on cotton and flax
                          system
        413   Weaving of cotton, linen and man-made fibres
        414   Woollen and worsted
        415   Jute
        416   Rope twine and net
        417   Hosiery and other knitted goods
        418   Lace
        419   Carpets
        420   Narrow fabrics
        422   Made-up textiles
        423   Textile finishing
        429   Other textile industries

                          Order XIV - Leather, Leather goods and Fur

        431   Leather and fellmongery
        432   Leather goods
        433   Fur

                          Order XV - Clothing and Footwear

        441   Weatherproof outerwear
        442   Men's and boy's tailored outerwear
        443   Women's and girl's tailored outerwear
        444   Overalls and men's shirts, underwear etc.
        445   Dresses, lingerie, infant's wear etc.
        446   Hats, caps and millinery
        449   Dress industries not elsewhere specified
        450   Footwear

                          Order XVIII - Timber, Furniture etc.

        471   Timber
        472   Furniture and upholstery
        473   Bedding etc.
        474   Shop and office equipment
        475   Wooden containers and baskets
        479   Miscellaneous wood and cork manufacturing

Minimum List Heading *	Order XXIII - Distributive Trades
810	Wholesale distribution of food and drink
811	Wholesale distribution of petroleum products
812	Other wholesale distribution
820	Retail distribution of food and drink
821	Other retail distribution
831	Dealing in coal, oil, builder's materials, grain and agricultural supplies
832	Dealing in other industrial materials and machinery

Order XXIV - Insurance, Banking and Finance

860	Insurance
861	Banking and bill discounting
862	Other financial institutions
863	Property owning and managing
864	Advertising and market research
865	Other business services
866	Central offices not allocatable elsewhere

Order XXV - Professional and scientific services

871	Accounting services
872	Educational services
873	Legal services
874	Medical and dental services
875	Religious organisations
876	Research and development services
879	Other professional and scientific services

Order XXVI - Miscellaneous services

881	Cinemas, theatres, radios etc.
882	Sport and other recreations
883	Betting and gambling
884	Hotels and other residential establishments
885	Restaurants, cafes, snack bars
886	Public houses
887	Clubs
888	Catering contractors
889	Hairdressing and manicure
891	Private domestic service
892	Laundries
893	Dry cleaning, job dying, carpet beating etc.
894	Motor repairers, distributors, garages and filling stations
895	Repair of boots and shoes
899	Other services

Minimum List Heading *   Order XXVII - Public Administration and
                          Defence

     901   National government service
     906   Local government service

* 'Minimum List Heading(s)' refer to component sub-categories of each
  Industrial Order.
Source: Central Statistical Office, Standard Industrial Classification
      1968, HMSO, 1968, pp. 1-6.

1.   FACTORS COMMON TO MOST LOW PAYING INDUSTRIES

Chapter 3 identified the characteristics of low paying industries but largely avoided explanation. The link between characteristics and causes is now discussed. A convenient starting point is to consider the relation to low pay of those characteristics found to be shared by most low paying industries, both manufacturing and service. The following six characteristics fall within this category: low paying industries generally contain large numbers of small firms and relatively few large firms; trade union density levels are relatively low; the incidence of wage drift is generally below average; average labour productivity is relatively low; capital/labour ratios are relatively low; and most low paying industries contain above average proportions of female employees.

A measure of the size or number of firms comprising industries is often employed as an indicator of the degree of competition within industries or product markets. Those industries dominated by a few large firms are assumed to be relatively free from competition. This, together with economies of scale, give them the opportunity to pay above average wages. In contrast, industries composed of many small firms producing similar products and services are supposed typically to be highly competitive. It is possible, therefore, that pay levels in low paying industries reflect the degree of competition in product markets. Monopoly profits and hence monopoly wages will be restricted.

Empirical tests of this proposition have produced inconclusive results. Most studies relate to the American economy. The independent influence of the degree of monopoly in an industry (as measured by concentration ratios) on wage movements (male manual) in United States manufacturing industries between 1947 and 1959 was measured by Bowen. It was noted that 'Apparently the existence of a relatively high degree of concentration in the product market can lead to above average wage increases in an industry even if the degree of unionization and profit level are only "average".' (1) Elsewhere, the correlation between wage levels and industrial concentration levels has been found to be low, implying that competitive factors alone provide an insufficient explanation for the existence of inter-industry differentials. (2)

The influence of firm size on pay levels is sometimes considered jointly with that of union density. Indeed, the two variables appear to be linked. As in low paying industries, low levels of concentration often coexist with weak trade unionism, while in concentrated sectors, trade unionism is generally strong. For all US manufacturing industry, Bowen calculated a correlation coefficient between the two variables of 0.46 (significant at the 5% level). In general, empirical evidence reveals a more positive association between pay levels and the combined influence of industrial concentration and union density. (3) Moreover, the combined impact of imperfections in both product and labour markets appears to be mutually reinforcing. Hence, Bowen's calculations implied that 'the joint effects of concentration and unionization may be greater than the algebraic sum of their individual effects'. (4) Similarly, the joint effects of low concentration and weak trade unionism were found to have a negatively reinforcing impact on pay levels.

Some association between low concentration levels and weak trade union organisation is to be expected. Problems of communication within the scattered small firm sector increase the effort and costs required of effective union recruitment activity. The competitive nature of product markets may also inhibit union growth, and indeed the wage-gaining ability of established unions, thereby accounting for the 'negative reinforcing effect' noted above. In an analysis relating to the US economy, Segal has argued that this is most likely to be the case where competitive industries operate in national markets. (5) Low entry barriers and the national market increase the ease of entry and exit of firms. Accordingly, there is a high propensity for locational shifts of industry either reflecting the migration of firms that search for low cost areas or firms that are 'running away' from unions. This limits the union's ability to evolve a wage policy that is relatively uninfluenced by intra-industry competitive pressures and creates the continuous danger of the growth of a non-union sector. Examples cited of competitive industries operating in national markets included apparel, leather, textiles and furniture - and arguably this typology approximates a number of British low paying industries, especially those in the manufacturing sector.

A low level of industrial concentration does not necessarily preclude the formation of strong unions, and some authors have pointed to instances where wage movements in certain industries (mainly non-manufacturing sectors) have been most favourable, where unions have been strong and where product markets have been highly competitive, for example, in construction, building and trucking (Rees), and in longshore, offshore, maritime and road trucking (Levinson). However, in these cases there are usually exceptional factors involved. With reference to Rees's findings, Segal observed that the industries concerned had state barriers on entry, a high degree of product differentiation, a high demand in the product market and were located in areas where the propensity to join unions was high. Similarly, Levinson noted that 'the spatial limitations of the physical area within which new entrants could effectively compete' constituted effective entry barriers in the competitive high wage industries he examined, in much the same way as did the degree of monopoly in high wage manufacturing industries. (6)

The coexistence of low concentration levels and weak unionism in low paying industries may further reflect the socio-psychological influence of the small firm environment on employee attitudes. Problems of communication and 'alienation' are said to be fewer in small firms. Management is more direct and flexible and working rules can be varied to suit the individual. Hence, 'the fact that small firms offer lower wages than large suggests that convenience of location, and generally the non-material satisfaction of working in them more than outweigh any financial sacrifice involved'. (7) If it is true that workers in small firms are generally less 'money motivated', and that the industrial relations climate is such that fewer grievances or problems arise, these factors may weaken the motivation or propensity to join trade unions. Some evidence of a relatively more peaceful industrial relations climate in small firms is implied by strike statistics. For the period 1971-73, for example, the percentage of total working days lost in manufacturing industry in the UK which were lost in small firms, expressed as a ratio of the percentage of total employees in manufacturing industry employed in small firms, was 0.2. Had the incidence of stoppages been proportionate to the employment size of the small firm sector, the ratio would have been 1.0. For intermediate firms the ratio was found to be 0.7 while in large firms the ratio was estimated as 2.0, indicating a disproportionately large number of days lost. (8)

The lesser incidence of wage drift in low paying industries implies a reliance, where unions exist at all, on national rather than local wage negotiating arrangements. This is certainly the case in national and local government and the NHS where unionism is relatively strong. Empirical evidence suggests, however, that it is only at the second tier of wage negotiations, at the level of the factory or plant, that unions have been able to secure for their members an earnings differential over workers in non-union plants. Employing earnings and union density data relating to 1964, Pencavel calculated that the 'relative wage effect' of trade unionism in the UK was in the order of 14% in those industries where local bargaining tended to prevail. In those industries not characterised by local bargaining, the relative wage effect was insignificant. (9) This implies that where trade unions exist in low paying industries, in terms of earnings, the institutional setting of collective bargaining renders them largely ineffectual. This may reflect the retarding influence of industry-wide bargaining on both union 'pushfulness' and on the freedom of management to evolve a wages policy conducive to local labour market conditions. (10)

The effects of low levels of productivity and capital intensity may now be added to the jigsaw. As was noted in the previous chapter, these variables are interlinked, and again, industrial levels of each appear to be related to the size of firms comprising industries. Nevertheless, even relative to the small firm sector generally, small firms in low paying industries were found to be unproductive and undercapitalised.

Assuming that low levels of average labour productivity reflect slower rates of productivity growth in the past, the apparent association between pay levels and productivity levels in low paying industries is, in theory, fairly simple to account for. Gains in productivity are said to permit some combination of higher pay, higher profits, lower costs, lower prices and, on occasions, new or improved products. A high rate of productivity growth thus enables a firm to offer higher wages while retaining prices at a favourable level. In relatively unproductive industries, these wages may be matched only at the expense of profit margins or price levels. Given, however, that low paying industries operate within a competitive environment, they will be more sensitive to price increases and are thus unlikely to match increases of earnings in more productive sectors. A low level of productivity or productivity growth will therefore impede a firm's 'ability to pay'. This is particularly likely where, in addition to low productivity, there is a high degree of labour intensity. The ratio of labour costs to total costs will be high and hence the demand for labour will be highly elastic. This in turn weakens employee bargaining power and strengthens employer resistence to wage increases.

The strength of the relationship between productivity and pay is, however, a matter of some debate. Empirical evidence is non-systematic and inconclusive, relating to different economies and time periods. Dunlop, for example, calculated a strong rank correlation between average hourly earnings and physical productivity changes for 33 US manufacturing industries between 1923 and 1940. (11) It was emphasised that this relationship was achieved despite the presence of many factors (e.g. differing capital/labour ratios, competitive conditions and skill mixes) which would, prima facie, tend to weaken the link between the two variables. In contrast, however, a British study by Salter found that movements in industrial productivity and earnings between 1925 and 1950 were generally uncorrelated. (12)

More recently, Jones, among others, has argued that the influence of industrial productivity on earnings is largely compromised through the effects of 'wage leadership'. (13) The economy, it is argued, is comprised of a leading sector and a following sector. The former usually consists of those industries with the fastest rates of productivity growth, where wages rise at more or less the same rate as productivity. Pressures are then set for similar increases in earnings in other less productive sectors: 'The rationale often given for this movement is economic, the market establishing a competitive rate; but the inspiration behind it is social and political: each feels entitled to the increase which others, particularly those near him, are seen to be getting'. (14) The general level of wage increase in the economy thus outstrips the average rate of productivity growth, thereby contributing to inflationary pressures.

The stability of the inter-industry wage structure which was observed in Chapter 2 is often cited as prima facie evidence of wage leadership. The model gains further empirical support from a wide-reaching study conducted by Turner and Jackson in 1970. Employing international data, the authors found that the general level of wages in various economies did tend to rise with output per head in the fastest growing industries. (15)

The relative stability of inter-industry differentials may, however, reflect factors other than wage leadership, and need not necessarily preclude an important relationship between productivity and pay, at least in the long run. Robinson and Macfarlane undertook a comprehensive analysis of changes in industrial earnings differentials (male manual workers) among 94 industries over the period 1948-69. (16) While the rank correlation for 1969 as against 1948 was calculated as 0.7, the authors found that ranking co-efficients declined as the time period used increased, suggesting a gradual but progressive movement from original rankings. Moreover, it was pointed out that even high rank correlations are consistent with considerable movements in industrial earnings rankings. These movements can on some occasions be quite dramatic. For example, coal mining ranked third out of 21 industrial groups in 1960 but twelfth in 1970. (17)

It is probable, in any case, that a number of the factors previously discussed (competitive environment, weak unions) have largely excluded low paying industries from the influence of any wage leadership forces which might exist, thereby strengthening the relation of productivity to pay. The sporadic insistence of recent incomes policies that earnings should rise only in line with increased productivity may also have strengthened this relationship and reduced the impact of wage leadership.

Low productivity may additionally be viewed as a supply-side phenomenon characterising individuals rather than industries. From this perspective, an individual's productivity level is said to be related to the amount of 'human capital' he possesses in terms of skill, training, education, innate ability and other such personal characteristics. Wages are viewed as analogous to an 'investment' by the employer in human capital. Accordingly, low wages are considered to reflect the low personal contribution or 'worth' of individual employees. (18)

Empirical evidence does show that the ranks of the low paid are strongly represented by large numbers of unskilled employees, the young and inexperienced, old employees possessing outmoded skills and reduced physical ability, the disabled and those in ill health. (19) With respect to industrial differences in pay and productivity, however, human capital theory is less convincing. For example, the previous chapter showed that a number of low paying manufacturing industries contained above average proportions of skilled employees. Moreover, as a broad generalisation, Bosanquet notes that the unskilled tend to be relatively high paid in manufacturing sectors and low paid in service sectors, implying that the industry in which a person is employed may be a more important determinant of pay than are individual characteristics. (20) This proposition was tested empirically in an American study by Wachtel and Betsey. (21) Employing multiple regression techniques, the authors' results appeared to show that the industry in which a person was employed was a more important determinant of individual earnings than were such personal characteristics as age, education, race, marital status and sex.

A final characteristic found to be common to most low paying industries is that they generally contain above average proportions of women. As with productivity levels, low earnings among women can be considered to reflect both the characteristics of the industries in which they are employed and the individual supply functions of female labour. As noted above, Wachtel and Betsey's study assigned primary explanatory importance to industry factors. However, this does not explain why women as a group should be overrepresented in those industries where the average earnings of men are lowest. In attempting to do so, it is perhaps misleading to view low pay as resulting from either 'industry' factors on the one hand, as opposed to 'individual' factors on the other, and to attempt to measure the relative importance of each set of factors. An examination of some of the supply and demand conditions affecting women's earnings suggests that the two sets of variables may be linked.

On the supply side, Chiplin and Sloane suggest that the two major factors which account for earnings differentials between men and women are: differences in labour force attachment; and differences in the type and extent of training. (22) In relation to the former, married women leave employment, not only to raise families, but because of geographical mobility on the part of the husband. In the case of single women, marital status is subject to alteration. As regards the latter, to the extent that an employer invests in specific training, the expected length of employment of an individual is important since it determines the rate of return on investment in 'human capital'. Lower wages for women may thus be viewed both as a means of increasing the net rate of return on their training, and compensation for their shorter expected duration of employment. In addition, however, the authors argue that these supply characteristics result in a large number of women being grouped into a separate labour market from most male employees where, on the demand side, their earnings are further depressed through the influence of a 'dual labour market'.

The notion of the dual labour market is American in origin, its applicability to Britain being first examined by Bosanquet and Doeringer. (23) The labour market is envisaged as comprising a 'primary' and a 'secondary' sector. The primary job market is characterised by high rates of productivity growth, high levels of skill and wages, employment stability and prospects of advancement, whereas the secondary labour market is characterised by low rates of productivity growth, low levels of skill and wages, little likelihood of promotion and high labour turnover. The authors attribute the existence of market duality to differential labour demand conditions within industries and firms. These in turn reflect differences in the internal manpower policies adopted by firms in each sector. The secondary labour market consists of firms having 'open' internal labour markets. Such firms hire workers directly into low paying jobs and provide little opportunity for promotion or training. In contrast, the primary sector consists of firms with 'structured' internal labour markets. These hire workers into a limited number of low paying entry jobs and then rely on training and promotion to staff the majority of remaining jobs. Hence 'it is the presence of enterprise-specific training on the demand-side of the labour market which encourages market duality'. (24)

Chiplin and Sloane suggest not only that supply factors associated with women's labour largely confine them to the secondary sector, but that 'a vicious circle may operate to perpetuate differences between the male and female occupational structure'. (25) For example, the growth of non-wage elements in labour costs in the primary market (e.g. training costs, recruitment and search costs) implies the need to minimize numbers and maximize hours in order to spread these costs which are fixed in relation to the number of employees. For women, this will make entry into the primary market even more difficult. For example, certain provisions of the Factories Acts impose restrictions on the amount and type of shift work which can be undertaken by women, and family responsibilities may preclude long overtime hours. Similarly, Bosanquet and Doeringer suggest that employment patterns in each sector tend to become self-reinforcing; 'Turnover occurs because there is no enterprise-specific training, and enterprise-specific training is inhibited by a turnover-prone disadvantaged workforce. In the primary sector opposite trends in workforce stability and specific training are likely'. (26)

The dual labour market hypothesis thus provides a link between 'individual'/'industry', supply/demand factors in accounting for low earnings among women. Sex need not be the only important variable. Other supply functions of the individual (e.g. education, age, race, health) may also help to account, via market duality, for the occupational and industrial pattern of low pay. Bosanquet and Doeringer suggest, however, that the distinction between primary and secondary markets is weaker in Britain than America. The usefulness of dual labour market theory in explaining the current pattern of low pay in Great Britain is more fully considered in the context of the sections which follow.

2. FACTORS PECULIAR TO LOW PAYING MANUFACTURING INDUSTRIES

In addition to the factors discussed above, low paying manufacturing industries were found to share a number of characteristics which differed both from those of higher paying manufacturing industries and those of low paying service industries. These were comprised in the main of differential trends in employment and productivity, and differences in occupational composition. Excepting timber, low paying manufacturing industries (and agriculture) substantially declined in employment between 1960 and 1973. The rate of decline far outstripped that of the manufacturing sector as a whole over this period. On the other hand, productivity growth in these industries was generally above the average manufacturing sector rate. As regards occupational composition, low paying manufacturing industries were generally found to contain below average proportions of unskilled manual workers and of administrative technical and clerical staff. The discussion which follows attempts to account for these characteristics and their relation to low pay.

Declining employment in an industry, in conjunction with low wages, implies an inadequacy of labour demand. This, in combination with a decrease in employee bargaining strength (owing to the threat of redundancy) has possibly contributed to low earnings in low wage manufacturing sectors. However, some explanation is required for the employment trends which have been observed.

As was noted in the previous chapter, employment in agriculture, mining, textiles and clothing industries has been declining since at least the beginning of the century. These movements reflect a number of fundamental structural changes to the traditional pattern of British industry which have occurred throughout this period. A notable feature of these developments has been the relative decline of the traditional craft and 'primary' sectors of the economy and the rapid expansion of capital-intensive science-based industries after the Second World War. In 1913, for example, coal and textiles together accounted for over 44% of British exports. In 1964 the proportion was only 7%. (27) Allen suggests that an important determinant of these changes was the rising price of raw materials following the Second World War:

'Whereas after 1920 raw materials were cheap, after 1945 they were dear, and the unfavourable terms of trade compelled the British to economise in imports. A strong inducement was therefore given to the production of synthetic materials, the manufacturing of which makes heavy demands on advanced technology and requires capital-intensive methods. Capital equipment was in effect substituted for land and materials through the application of modern technology'. (28)

Changing product demand conditions in the home market, resulting from steadily rising incomes and changing tastes, may have further contributed to the relative decline of agriculture and low wage manufacturing industries. Between 1948 and 1977, average post tax income per head in Britain doubled in real terms. (29) Food and clothing products tend, however, to have relatively low income elasticities of demand. Consequently, as incomes have risen, the share of agriculture, textiles and clothing industries in aggregate demand has steadily declined. Further, a low price elasticity of demand has possibly limited the growth of product sales in these industries.

An important difference between low paying manufacturing and low paying service industries lies in the nature of their respective product markets. It was suggested in the previous section that British low paying manufacturing industries, like their American counterparts, generally served national markets and that indirectly this could weaken the effectiveness of trade union organisation. However, not only are markets national; they tend also to be international in contrast to low wage service sectors which, apart from hotels, predominantly serve local markets. Low pay and declining employment in manufacturing sectors may therefore be additionally linked to trends in international competition.

The striking similarity of low wage manufacturing industries internationally gains some support for this proposition. An American study by Stewart, for example, identified as low wage industries, (at the US three-digit level of analysis), textiles, apparel, lumber and wood products, furniture and fixtures and leather and leather products. (30) This similarity may in part reflect similar technological processes and production techniques common to those industries internationally, and further suggests that structural developments in the British and American economies have been similar. Stewart, however, regards declining employment and low pay in textiles and apparel, and to a lesser extent in leather and lumber industries 'to be increasingly a function of the level of protection from imports'. (31)

It is not possible to provide a precise index of the competitive position of British low paying industries in world markets. Import-export statistics relate to products rather than to SIC industry groupings. A number of textile products appear, nevertheless, to have fared relatively badly. Between 1958 and 1968, production of woven cotton and man-made fibres decreased from 2,362 to 1,622 million square yards. Exports decreased from 468 to 227 million square yards while imports increased from 434 to 854 million square yards. (32)

Some rough indication of 'international competitiveness' by broad industry groupings can perhaps be obtained by comparing concentration levels. Glyn and Sutcliffe argue that the British merger boom between 1964 and 1970 occurred primarily in response to an intensification of international competition from the mid-1960s. The extension of monopolies in export industries enabled higher prices to be charged and production to be rationalised and restructured, thereby offsetting pressure on profit margins. (33) The continuing dominance of small firms in low paying industries thus suggests their relative vulnerability to international competitive pressures.

Competitive vulnerability, in conjunction with the recent inten- sification of international competition, may account for the particularly rapid decline in employment in low paying manufacturing industries from the mid-1960s. This will in part reflect the increasing bankruptcy rate for small inefficient firms. In the period 1964-69 the average number of bankruptcies per year was double the average rate for the preceding decade. (34) Bearing in mind, however, that these employment trends were not generally associated with decreases in output, but rather with average or above average increases in productivity, at least part of the decline may be attributed to increases in investment and capital restructuring programmes which have resulted in technological displacement of labour. The merger boom did not by-pass low paying industries. In 1957, eight companies owned 50% of the assets in textiles. By 1968, the number had been reduced to three. (35) Declining employment in these industries can therefore be viewed both as consequence of, and as a response to, international competitive pressures. To a lesser extent, this holds true for the production or industry sector as a whole which, from the mid-1960s (and for the first time in post-war history), began to decline absolutely in employment.

The movements discussed above can in some part account for the occupational and skill patterns observed for low paying manufacturing industries. Braverman has argued that the proportions of admini- strative, professional and clerical employees tend to increase relative to other occupational categories as industries become more concentrated, owing in particular to the increasing duplication of accounting and record-keeping procedures which apparently becomes necessary as companies increase in size. (36) Hence the lower proportions of these occupational categories in low paying industries may simply reflect lower concentration levels. Similarly, as suggested in the previous chapter, the higher proportions of skilled employees in these industries may reflect a lower priority accorded to the unskilled in times of redundancies. This view gains some support from Table 4.1 which shows from 1959, a relatively larger decrease in employment for women than for men in low paying manufacturing industries. Bearing in mind the earlier finding that low paying manufacturing industries employ relatively few part-time women, these figures suggest a shake-out of the least skilled sector of the

64.

workforce. Alternatively (or additionally) the figures might indicate a degree of sexual discrimination in the redundancy policies of employers.

TABLE 4.1   Decline in Employment from Low Wage Manufacturing Industries – Men and Women, 1959-73 (thousands)

	1959	1973	Absolute decrease	% Decrease
Textiles, leather, clothing, footwear				
Men	519	427	- 92	-17.7%
Women	825	590	-235	-28.0%

Source: Department of Employment Gazette, March 1975, op.cit., Table 5, pp. 197-202.

As has been pointed out, the above average proportions of skilled manual employees in low wage manufacturing sectors question the general validity of human capital theories of wage determination. Moreover, the mass exodus of women from these industries and the above average skill levels of remaining employees, (including women), imply changing labour market conditions which bear a decreasing resemblance to those of a secondary sector as depicted in the dual labour market hypothesis.

Summing up, unfavourable labour and product market conditions appear to be factors of particular importance in accounting for low earnings levels in low paying manufacturing industries. These conditions reflect the unfavourable influence of a number of structural changes and developments in the British economy, which have occurred in response to the rising prices of raw material imports, rising incomes and changing tastes in the home market and more recently in response to the intensification of international competition.

3.   FACTORS PECULIAR TO LOW PAYING SERVICE INDUSTRIES

In contrast to low paying manufacturing industries, low paying service industries generally expanded in employment over the period examined. This was accompanied by average or marginally above average rates of growth in output while rates of growth in productivity were generally below average. In the 1970s large areas of the service sector experienced negative productivity growth. In addition, it has been observed that the employment of full-time and part-time women (employees among whom the incidence of low pay was found to be greatest) is largely confined to these industries. (37) The skill levels of service employees also appeared to be relatively low. Finally, the earnings of male manual employees in low paying service industries were found to be tied relatively closely to basic pay, reflecting in the main the relatively small contribution which PBR payments made to total earnings. This section seeks to account for these characteristics and to clarify their possible relation to the development, prevalence and persistence of low pay in the service sector of the economy.

A.   Service industries as a secondary labour market

Of the characteristics described above, low productivity growth, low skill levels and the strong representation of women are factors which imply a strong similarity of labour market conditions in low paying service industries to those of a secondary labour market as described in Section 1. It has been observed, for example, that the manpower policies adopted by employers in the secondary market are assumed to offer little scope for promotion or training. This certainly seemed to be the case in large shops where some 70% of workers were employed in low skill/low authority jobs. The lower job and educational qualifications possessed by women, relative to men, also suggested the lesser training or skill requirements of service occupations. A further feature of manpower policy in the secondary sector is that a lesser reliance is assumed to be placed on shift work and overtime, since non-wage costs in labour costs (recruitment costs, search costs, training costs) are relatively small. This again accords with what has been observed. For women generally, overtime and shift payments were found to contribute very little to total earnings. Similarly, these components were of less than average importance in the make-up of manual men's earnings in a number of low paying service industries, particularly in miscellaneous services (Table 3.13).

Table 3.13 showed that this last characteristic (the lower incidence of shift work and overtime) applied equally to a number of low paying manufacturing industries, though it has been observed that in other respects (e.g. skill levels, recent trends in productivity) low paying service industries better fit the description of the secondary market than do low paying manufacturing industries. Additional evidence that this is so is implied by comparative data on rates of labour turnover by industry. Turnover rates in the secondary market are assumed to be relatively high. Table 4.2 provides estimates of labour turnover in both low paying manufacturing and low paying service industries for 1974. The indicator of labour turnover employed (proportion of total employees with under 12 month's service with current employer) is that which is commonly used by the Department of Employment in comparing turnover rates among broad groups of industries. The figures show that while turnover rates, as so measured, were above average in most low paying industries, they were generally higher in low paying service industries (other than public administration) (38) than in low paying manufacturing industries. The highest rates occurred in miscellaneous services and the distributive trades where approximately 30% of total employees in each industry had been engaged by their current employer for under 12 months.

The apparent similarity of labour market conditions in low paying service industries to those of a secondary labour market does not, in itself, explain the development or prevalence of low pay in the service sector of the economy. A fuller account requires to consider further the nature of the relation between labour market duality or 'segmentation' and differential earnings levels and to offer some explanation as to why service industries in particular have developed the features of the secondary market.

TABLE 4.2   Labour Turnover in Selected Industries: Proportions of Total Employees who had been Employed with their Current Employer for Less Than 12 Months in April 1974

Industry	Proportions employed for less than 12 months (%)
All industries and services	22.6
All manufacturing industries	20.6
Textiles	22.4
Clothing and footwear	23.3
Leather, leather goods and fur	22.2
Timber, furniture etc.	23.8
Distributive trades	29.1
Insurance, banking and finance	26.6
Professional and scientific services	24.3
Miscellaneous services	30.0
Public administration and defence	18.0

Source: _Department of Employment Gazette_, January 1975, p. 25; _Department of Employment Gazette_, September 1975, p. 894.

Orthodox competitive theory has long recognised segmentation of the labour market as a cause of inequality and low pay. The relation has traditionally been perceived as one of imperfections in the smooth operation of the labour market which limit the mobility of workers between differing occupations, industries or sectors of the economy, thus preventing the equalisation of wages or the 'net advantages' of different jobs through the operation of market forces. From this perspective, barriers to mobility arise through factors 'exogenous' to the economic system such as misinformation, geographical immobility or the imperfect 'interchangeability' of skills. Recognition of this last factor led to the 19th century notion of 'non-competing groups' as developed by Cairnes as an explanation for segmentation, labour immobility and differential earnings. (39) The notion rested on the premise that persons of differing skills or qualifications, for example, plumbers and doctors, did not compete in the same labour market and that in the short-run, the earnings of possessors of skills which were relatively scarce could contain an element of 'quasi-rent'; though a long-run tendency to its elimination was assumed, through the attraction of new entrants to acquire the necessary skills.

More recent theories which have continued the methodology of classical or neo-classical orthodoxy have built on Cairnes's model and sought to explain the prolongation of segmentation and inequality through the more permanent effects of social class or inherited social and political inequality, where children are largely confined to the same segment of the labour market as their parents, (40) or through the effects of 'non-economic' racial or sexual discrimination, which raise further barriers to mobility, barriers which become more resilient in a world of prejudice and imperfect information, where participants beliefs can become self-justifying. (41)

A common criticism of these later approaches is that they fail to explain adequately the origins of social or political barriers to mobility. Again these tend to be treated as exogenous to the model, as aberrations within an otherwise harmonious system. This, it has been argued, weakens the analytical or explanatory value of orthodox competitive theory. (42) Moreover, while providing some useful insights into the determinants of earnings inequality in general, or between differentiated groups of individuals, the competitive model fails to account fully for the industrial pattern of labour market segmentation, and in particular its development broadly in line with the 'industry'/service division.

It is with respect to these limitations that Bosanquet and Doeringer's model of market duality is perhaps more illuminating. Within this model (as originally and more fully elaborated in an earlier work by Doeringer and Piore) (43) segmentation and low earnings again reflect barriers to mobility. Unlike competitive theory, however, Doeringer and Piore suggest that these barriers are themselves <u>generated</u> by technological and structural developments in the economy, that is, they are 'endogenous' to the economic system.

Dual labour markets arose, it is argued, because of relative advances in technology in the primary, 'core' or 'industry' sector of the economy. The rapid growth of capital-intensive, science-based industries, which was commented upon in the previous section, led to an ever-increasing reliance on technology-specific and enterprise-specific skills. Since the provision of these was costly in terms of training or search costs, labour turnover needed to be reduced. The large capital outlays which were necessary to finance the complex production techniques and developing technology in the primary sector enhanced the importance of a relatively stable workforce, as interruptions to the work process were very costly and production required to be maintained consistently at full capacity. To induce stability, employers thus developed and relied on a 'structured' internal manpower policy as described in Section 1. High wages and prospects of advancement were offered by restricting the number of 'ports of entry', to each of which a promotion ladder was attached, with promotion largely determined by seniority. In the secondary sector, on the other hand, where technology was relatively stagnant and inducements to stability were unnecessary or even disadvantageous in cost terms, employers preferred to pursue an 'open' manpower policy and recruited freely from the external market. The effects of these divergent policies on labour mobility were two-fold. First, mobility <u>between</u> the secondary and primary sectors was reduced, thereby increasing competition for jobs in the former and holding down wages. Second, the existence of promotion ladders and seniority provisions restricted mobility <u>within</u> the primary sector so that competition for high paying posts was reduced. The net effect was to depress general wage levels in the secondary sector relative to those in the primary sector.

The Doeringer-Piore model implies, therefore, that the industrial pattern of segmentation and low pay may be technologically determined.

This is not an implausable explanation. A number of service industries
are, by their very nature, less susceptible to technological change
or machinery-induced improvements to productivity or output. Personal
attention or contact is often a more important element in the
provision of a service than is technological sophistication, so that
in order to operate effectively, many service industries require, by
necessity, to retain a labour-intensive low-technology profile.
Accordingly, service industries do tend to rely to a lesser extent on
enterprise-specific or technology-specific skills. Indeed, often the
'skills' required of service occupations are those already possessed
by large sectors of the population and attained outside the labour
market, either through the education system (basic numeracy or
literacy), or, among women in particular, those learned in the home,
(catering skills, cleaning or other domestic skills). The more
limited scope for technological improvements in service industries,
and hence the lesser necessity for large capital outlays and expensive
training programmes, may thus reduce or negate the cost benefit to
service employers of inducing labour stability through a policy of
high wages and advantageous job prospects.

As has been pointed out, the Doeringer-Poire model does not accord
well with the characteristics observed of low paying manufacturing
industries. While exhibiting most of the features of the secondary
market (low wages, high proportions of women, fairly high labour
turnover), these industries nevertheless appeared to contain below
average proportions of unskilled workers. While challenging the
general applicability of the model, this finding does not, however,
necessarily undermine its basic premises. The previous section has
described how low paying manufacturing industries have been subject
to exceptionally unfavourable demand conditions in both product and
labour markets. Under these circumstances the motivation or necessity
to reduce mobility among skilled workers may be diminished. Indeed, a
more rational employer response might be to encourage labour mobility
through low wages, so as to achieve necessary reductions in labour
through 'natural wastage', thereby avoiding costly redundancy payments.
The high proportions of skilled employees remaining in these
industries may, as previously suggested, reflect discriminatory
redundancy policies in favour of the skilled; or alternatively may
reflect the lesser willingness of skilled workers to seek new jobs,
particularly if skills are of a type specific to the industry and
becoming obsolete. Opportunities for alternative employment may be few
and possibly restricted to even lower paying unskilled occupations.
(44)

A more fundamental challenge to the model is contained in Braverman's
recent analysis. Contrary to dual labour market theory, Braverman
suggests that the development of technology and the introduction of
scientific management techniques under 'monopoly capitalism' have
progressively reduced, rather than increased a worker's control over
his work process and hence his skill, where skill is defined as the
ability and opportunity to use knowledge and exercise judgement. In
this process, general craft skills were reduced to job-specific
skills, but further developments in technology and work organisation
in turn reduced job-specific skills:

'The more science is incorporated into the labor process,
the less the worker understands of the process; the more
sophisticated an intellectual product the machine becomes,
the less control and comprehension of the machine the
worker has. In other words, the more the worker needs to
know in order to remain a human being at work, the less
does he or she know'. (45)

This 'deskilling process', it is argued, has progressed furthest in
the concentrated industry sector of the economy where the division of
labour and machinery-related production techniques are most fully
developed, though the service sector has by no means been exempt.
Indeed, Braverman argues that in more recent years it is in certain
service industries that advances in technology and changes in work
organisation have been most rapid, resulting in similar reductions in
skill levels. (46) The net effect has been a general reduction in
skill levels in all sectors of the economy and the progressive
homogenisation of the labour force, particularly over the post-war
period, as opposed to a polarization of skills as argued by Doeringer
and Piore.

The implications of Braverman's analysis for dual market theory have
been considered by Rubery. (47) Rubery criticises the Doeringer-Piore
model on the ground that developments in technology and economic
structure are viewed from only one perspective: through the
motivations and actions of employers. Rubery additionally incorporates
the role of trade unions into dual labour market theory and substitutes trade unions for employers as the main agents through which
segmented labour markets are developed.

Segmented labour markets develop, it is argued, primarily through
the defensive action of trade unions to protect wage levels and jobs
in the light of the progressive deskilling and homogenisation of
labour brought about by technological change. Technological advances
throughout the 20th century both created new bargaining opportunities
for previously unorganised groups of workers and at the same time
threatened the basis of existing trade union organisation. On the one
hand, the advent of machine technology transformed many labouring jobs
into operating jobs where workers were in direct contact with
machinery and thus exercised some control over a greater output than
their own unassisted labour could achieve, thereby creating improved
bargaining opportunities for the mass of workers. On the other hand,
the deskilling process associated with the new technology threatened
to undermine the power base of existing unions whose strength lay in
the ability of craftsmen in manufacturing industry to use their
specialised knowledge as a means of organisation and to control entry
into their craft. This threat provoked a number of defensive
strategies on the part of unions aimed at maintaining the privileged
position of craft workers and combating increasing competition in the
labour market. In some cases, craft unions where sufficiently strong
to withstand the obsolescence of skills on which they had been based,
through, for example, the insistence on lengthy apprenticeship schemes
or high entry qualifications. More commonly, however, Rubery argues
that trade union organisation adapted and restructured itself around
the new machine technology, extending membership to 'semi-skilled' and

'unskilled' groups whilst maintaining a structured, sheltered labour market based on control of entry. For example, the case of the UK shipbuilding industry is cited, where craft unions forestalled the threat of dilution, (the substitution of unskilled and semi-skilled for skilled workers), by amalgamations with other unions representing lesser but possibly competing skills, and later insisted on apprenticeships as the only means of entry into the industry, so that few new operations were free to be taken up by unskilled employees from the open market. Similarly, Rubery describes how in engineering, the shop stewards' movement realised the seriousness of the dilution threat, and attempted not only to preserve craft control, but also to develop organisation in all grades, along with an industrial, rather than a craft policy on wages and labour supply.

Segmented labour markets and low pay result, therefore, from barriers to mobility set up by trade unions rather than employers, as a response to the diminution rather than the enhancement of skill levels demanded by technology. Mobility is reduced by means of apprenticeship systems, demarcation lines and the maintenance of obsolete or creation of artificial skill distinctions, which reduce competition and maintain wage levels and job stability in the unionised sector to the detriment of the unorganised sector. Again, however, these barriers are not viewed as exogenous influences on labour market structure. Rather, worker organisation attempts to control the competition in the labour market that the economic system generates, and adapts and restructures itself in response to developments in the economic structure.

Rubery's analysis thus implies that the industrial pattern of segmentation and low pay is determined by the relative scope for trade union organisation and development in differing sectors of the economy, an explanation consistent with the low union density levels observed in most low paying industries, and one which allows low paying manufacturing industries to be incorporated more easily within dual labour market theory. Like the Doeringer-Poire model, however, the primary or underlying explanation would appear again to lie in uneven developments in technology and industrial structure among industries and between different sectors of the economy. It is probable, for example, that the slower growth of machinery-related production techniques in service industries has been a major impediment to the development of strong trade unionism and hence an important factor contributing to low earnings, especially in distribution and miscellaneous services where trade unionism is virtually non-existent. Similarly, low paying industries, (service industries in particular), appear to have remained relatively uninfluenced by the general trend towards increasing concentration of production, and the discussion in Section 1 has suggested some ways in which this may have inhibited the development and effectiveness of trade unionism.

B.   Growth in employment

The relation of employment growth to low pay in service industries is perhaps best understood following an account of the factors giving rise to the employment trends observed.

Table 3.6 of the previous chapter showed that public sector service industries were among those which experienced the largest increase in employment over the period examined. Employment in public administration and defence, incorporating national and local government services, increased by some 23% between 1960 and 1973, while employment in professional and scientific services (mainly composed of employees in education and the NHS) grew over the same period by almost 60%. This expansion appears to reflect a policy of ever-increasing public expenditure in post-war Britain. Expressed as a percentage of GDP, total general government expenditure rose from 40% in 1954 to over 50% in 1978. (48) One of the main areas of growth in both employment and expenditure has been in 'social services', a category composed of education, health and personal social services and social security. For example, social services expenditure rose from 13% of GDP in 1951 to 21% in 1971. This represented a rise from 29% to 42% of total public expenditure. (49) Indeed, the real value of health benefits accruing to households increased by 5% each year on average between 1961 and 1975. (50)

A variety of explanations have been advanced for these trends. Hobsbawm, for example, suggests that the suffering and sacrifices incurred by the British population during World War II gave rise to high expectations of the post-war period, expectations which swept Labour to power at the 1945 general election and secured widespread support for the social and expansionist policies of the post-war Labour administration. The initial expansion of public services and the rise of the welfare state also owed much to 'the new Keynesian economics which rapidly infiltrated government through the massive recruitment of academics and other outsiders into the civil service'. (51)

Parkin, on the other hand, argues that the growth in public employment and welfare expenditure cannot be wholly attributed to the policies of social democratic governments. Employing international data, he shows that Western European countries which had been dominated by Right or Centre post-war governments did not, by 1960, allocate a smaller share of their resources to welfare than did countries dominated by governments of the Left. Instead, it is argued that the initial expansion of welfare benefits to the less privileged strata took place to damp down revolutionary movements in the immediate post-war period. In Germany, for example, 'The introduction of social security legislation by Bismarck ... was quite an explicit attempt to undermine the growing appeal of Marxian socialism among the German working class'. (52) A further reason was 'economic'. Workers who enjoy good health, housing and basic education are more productive than those who live in squalor, ignorance or disease.

Some explanation for the rapid and continuing growth in public employment throughout the 1960s and early 1970s is offered by Yaffe. (53) Like Parkin, Yaffe attributes the initial expansion of welfare services to a combination of working class pressure, the demands of industry for a relatively healthy workforce educated in basic skills at least, and the need for government to maintain employment levels at a politically tolerable level in order to gain union support for its policies and to ensure social and political stability. Yaffe argues, however, that the growth of expenditure and employment in the state sector, (excluding the nationalised industries and a small proportion of expenditure on education and health) was largely 'non-productive' in the sense that it required to be financed indirectly from private industry and hence was a drain on profits. To cope with this expense, and in order to maintain profit rates, productivity in the private and nationalised sectors required to be increased (as witnessed by the rise of productivity bargaining in the mid-1960s). One effect of this was the technological displacement of large numbers of workers from the industry sector of the economy, a process which contributed a further impetus to the expansion of non-productive public employment, thus again increasing pressure on profit margins. (54) Hence a vicious circle ensued whereby to maintain full employment conditions and offset (temporarily) the 'latent crisis conditions' inherent in the capital accumulation process, public services required to increase constantly their share of total employment. This explanation applies not only to Britain. Similar developments were thought to have occurred in most major post-war capitalist economies.

Outside the public sector, the largest increase in employment occurred in insurance, banking, financial and commercial-type services. Accounting and legal services (included under professional and scientific services in SIC 1968) may also be considered as part of this group. The growth of employment in these services can largely be attributed to the post-war expansion of credit. The rate of growth of credit has been startling, particularly in recent years. For example, over a comparatively short period, total bank advances in Britain increased by a factor of almost six from £7,536 million in 1967 to £42,728 million in 1975. (55) There was a particularly sharp increase in government borrowing. Expressed as a percentage of GDP, the public sector borrowing requirement increased from 2.8% in 1971 to 11.4% in 1975. (56) Again this trend appears to be international. In the United States, total private debt increased from 73% of GNP in 1946 to 149% in 1945. State and local government debt over the same period rose from 6.5% of GNP to 14.2%. (57)

Yaffe again views this expansion as a necessary feature of the full employment boom conditions of post-war market economies. Increases in state expenditure required to be financed from an extension of national debt, thus resulting in the rapid growth of the credit base of banks and other financial institutions. The expansion of credit was also required in order to bring about the necessary restructuring and concentration of capital, and competitive increases to the productivity of labour, factors vital in stimulating the expansion of production and offsetting the tendency for stagnation.

Employment growth in the miscellaneous group of small and pre-dominantly private service industries including catering, hair-dressing, laundries and entertainment is a continuation of pre-war trends and appears to have resulted from factors similar to those which contributed to the decline of low paying manufacturing industries. Income elasticity of demand for goods is slightly less than for services. As incomes have risen, a higher proportion of the increase has therefore been spent on services than goods. Further, the relatively slow rates of productivity growth in these industries, combined with the difficulties experienced in raising productivity have prohibited the expansion of output other than by means of an increase in employment. (58)

In distribution, employment growth appears to have levelled off over the latter half of the post-war period, following a general expansion since at least 1930. (59) Nevertheless, in 1976, the distributive trades continued to occupy the highest position, in employment terms, of all industries in SIC 1968. In reference to the American economy, Stewart has argued that since the income elasticity of demand for goods is less than for services, the distributive trades, more than other services, has depended for its long term growth in employment 'on its slow growth in productivity relative to the growth of productivity in goods producing industries'. (60)

Post-war developments giving rise to increased labour demand in service industries appear at the same time to have generated additional sources of supply. Labour displaced from industry represents one additional source, not only for the public services but for the service sector generally. The previous chapter also noted the large influx of women into service industries and the changing sexual composition of service employment. This possibly reflects the expansion of economic activity into what was formerly 'domestic production', normally carried out by women in the home. The growth of laundries, hair-dressing and catering establishments are examples. The expansion of a number of state services (health care, education, social services) may also have reduced the family responsibilities of women. A further factor has been the growth of labour saving devices in the home. By 1978 in Britain, 91% of households contained a refrigerator, 75% a washing machine and 92% a vacuum cleaner. (61) Rising family aspirations over the post-war period may have further encouraged the increasing participation of women in the labour market.

Though difficult to confirm statistically, a further source of labour which service industries have relied on for expansion has been immigrant. Stephen notes that the greatest influx of immigrants into Britain occurred in response to active government encouragement during the 1950s and 1960s when labour markets were tight and public utilities undermanned. Hence large numbers were drawn into transport services, public cleansing and hospital ancillary work. (62) The Low Pay Unit has also noted the high concentrations of foreign and immigrant labour in the hotel and catering trades. (63) Braverman argues that supplies of foreign labour are generated through the need for capitalist economies to expand across national boundaries in order to maintain profit rates. This process of imperialist penetration disturbs traditional forms of labour and subsistence, thus expanding the pool of former agricultural labour which may be drawn upon from the colonies and neo-colonies. (64)

The implications of these developments for the analysis of low pay may now be considered.

Two important features of the growth of public services, as far as wage levels are concerned, are first, that it has largely been a growth in wage costs; and second, rising public expenditure has been largely 'non-productive' in the sense employed by Yaffe above. The former feature reflects the labour intensity of public employment, which in turn reflects the degree of personal attention required of such services (education, health care), and the prohibitive cost of increasing productivity and 'output' in these areas through programmes of capital investment. Indeed, in the UK, the number of hospital beds per 1,000 population actually declined from 10.6 in 1950 to 9.00 in 1975. (65) On the other hand, by 1976, wage costs represented some 53% of total costs in local government (66) and over 70% of total expenditure in health and personal social services. (67) The high proportion of labour costs to total cost, together with the 'non-productive' or 'wealth-consuming' nature of these services are factors which explain why government policies, particularly recent income policies, have borne relatively heavily on wage levels in this sector. An additional explanation for this phenomenon is that governments have restricted the growth of public sector pay in order to encourage lower pay settlements elsewhere in the economy. (68)

With respect to the service sector as a whole, the link between employment growth and low pay is most often considered from the supply side of the labour market. A common view is that the 'release' of women and ethnic minorities onto the labour market, together with shrinking employment opportunities outside the service sector, has contributed to a glut or 'oversupply' of labour in service industries, thereby increasing competition for jobs and depressing wages. From this viewpoint, oversupply reflects not only the increasing availability of labour but that employment growth has been very rapid and subject to little trade union control. This in turn may reflect the lower propensity of women, ethnic minorities and other disadvantaged groups to join trade unions and the difficulties noted earlier of establishing and maintaining effective trade union organisation in service industries, at least in those outside the public sector.

Indeed, far from protecting the earnings of service employees, Rubery argues that the response of trade unions to post-war changes in the composition and distribution of employment may have further contributed to the formation and perpetuation of segmented labour markets, thus exacerbating competitive conditions for service workers. This occurs, it is argued, because workers previously at the bottom of the job structure take advantage of the new supplies of labour to move up the hierarchy, and at the same time tend to organise to protect themselves against the increased competition. Similarly, Rubery suggests that the substitution of women for men in an industry can lead to a decline in male earnings and reduces employment opportunities for men; hence the incentive for men (or male-dominated trade unions) to confine women to a different segment of the labour market. Or again, the decline in the share of typically high paying industries in total employment may increase the incentive for workers in those sectors to differentiate themselves, thus reinforcing existing barriers between primary and secondary sectors. (69)

Braverman links the growth of employment in service industries to low pay via the Marxian notion of the rise of the 'industrial reserve army of labour'. This 'army' of surplus labour is said to grow in direct proportion to the extent and energy of the capital accumulation process, bringing about 'an accumulation of misery corresponding with the accumulation of capital' and leading ultimately to the pauperization of the mass of workers. For Braverman, the growth of the reserve army is represented by the increasing participation of female and immigrant labour in post-war capitalist economies, and in particular, by those workers 'sloughed off' from production industries

through mechanisation according to that process described by Yaffe.
The pauperization process is illustrated by the relative expansion of
the service sector of post-war capitalist economies, and, according
to evidence relating to the American economy, by a simultaneous
decline in the earnings of service workers relative to those of
production workers. (70)

The growth of the reserve army contributes to this process through
its influence on both supply and demand conditions in service labour
markets. First, wages in service industries are held down through
oversupply as discussed above. Second, on the demand-side, Braverman
argues that the continuous availability of surplus labour has
encouraged service employers to adopt, invest in and thus expand those
labour-intensive production techniques and forms of the labour process
which may only operate profitably through a low-wage employment
policy, so that the demand for labour in post-war capitalist economies
has increasingly been a demand for cheap, low wage hand labour. Hence
the tendency for an increasing portion of the labour force to 'pile
up' in the lowest paying service sectors of the economy:

'The paradox that the most rapidly growing mass occupations in
an era of scientific-technical revolution are those which
have least to do with science and technology need not surprise
us. The purpose of machinery is not to increase but to decrease
the numbers of workers attached to it. Thus it is by no means
illogical that with the development of science and technology,
the numbers of those cheaply available for dancing attendance
upon capital in all of its least mechanized functional forms
continues to increase at a rapid pace'. (71)

For Britain, data limitations make it difficult to assess whether
the post-war expansion of service industries has been accompanied by
an actual fall in the earnings of service workers relative to those
of production workers. Certainly, the influence of the structural
changes described on both supply and demand conditions in service
industries has contributed at least to the persistence of low pay, and
at the same time has increasingly altered the industrial pattern of
low pay to that of a service sector phenomenon. Among British authors,
this change is often referred to as one in the 'typicality' of the low
paid employee: 'Before the First World War, the typical low paid
worker was employed in a declining handcraft industry. Now the
typical low paid worker is a porter in a hotel, clerk or shop
assistant'. (72)

C.   Payment by results

The systems or methods of wage payment characterising service
industries may additionally contribute to low earnings. In particular,
the relatively small contribution which PBR payments make to the
earnings of male manual workers implies that service employees are
afforded relatively few opportunities to enhance low basic pay or
boost earnings through improvements in individual (or group) effort
or performance. This seemed to be the case in all low paying service
industries other than public administration, but not in low paying

manufacturing industries (Table 3.13). In the latter, PBR payments represented a relatively important source of earnings, especially in clothing and footwear and timber, though any earnings advantages afforded by such schemes appeared to be largely offset by lower opportunities for overtime and shift working. (73)

The wider use of PBR schemes in public administration, relative to other service industries, reflects the emphasis which the NBPI placed on the introduction of bonus incentive schemes as a solution to low pay among local authority manual workers. In October 1966, only some 16% of these employees were covered by such schemes which accounted on average for just 3% of their total pay. In the Board's view, this situation not only contributed directly to low pay, by limiting the earnings opportunities of workers, but also indirectly by limiting worker motivation or incentive to improve efficiency or productivity. The wider use of bonus incentive schemes was thus recommended and by April 1976 over 70% of manual men in local authorities were covered by such schemes which, on average, made up 13% of their total earnings. This appears to have contributed to an improvement in the relative pay position of these employees whose earnings, expressed as a percentage of average male manual earnings, increased from 76.3% in October 1966 to 87.2% in April 1976. (74)

It is sometimes argued that the wide use of PBR schemes in an industry not only enhances the earnings opportunities of workers covered by these schemes but may also confer benefits on workers on alternative systems of payment. For example, McCormick notes that in UK engineering, increases in the earnings of pieceworkers arising from increased productivity tend to lead to similar increases in the earnings of timeworkers. This is because timeworkers use the earnings of pieceworkers as a bargaining base to 'bid-up' time-rates. Moreover, the frequent disturbance of differentials between timeworkers and pieceworkers continually generates pressures for a new wage round or wage spiral, a process which benefits all employees in the industry. (75) In service industries, where piecework is less common (and trade unions weaker) this process is less likely to occur.

Again, however, the lower reliance on PBR schemes in service industries may itself be considered a function of technology and developments in industrial structure. For example, the lesser reliance on machinery in the service sector means that there are difficulties in defining and measuring the output of a service, so that pay is not easily related to performance. The size of firms may also be of importance. Lydall notes that the proportion of workers on piecework systems tends to decrease with the size of establishments and that in establishments of less than 10 workers (not uncommon in the service sector) PBR systems are extremely difficult to operate and hence virtually non-existent. (76)

4. SUMMARY AND CONCLUSIONS

This chapter has applied a number of perspectives to a complex phenomenon. The discussion has suggested some ways in which low pay may be related to those characteristics shared by most low paying industries, but, in addition, has shown that to a considerable extent the causes of low pay in low paying manufacturing industries differ

from those relating to low paying service industries. Some attempt
has been made to account for the differing characteristics of each
sector and to explain their relation to low pay through reference to
developments in technology and economic structure. The main
conclusions are summarised below:

1. Factors common to most low paying industries The analysis in
    Section 1, and the empirical evidence cited in support, suggest
    that characteristics are not related to causes in a simple or
    direct sense. Rather, a strong theme has been the apparent inter-
    dependence of the factors discussed and their mutually
    reinforcing impact on earnings levels. For example, it has been
    argued that low levels of industrial concentration may contribute
    both directly to low pay, by restricting the payment of monopoly
    wages, and indirectly by inhibiting the development and
    effectiveness of trade unionism. The effectiveness of trade
    unionism may be further restricted by the predominance of
    national wage negotiating arrangements (as implied by the low
    incidence of wage drift). Weak trade union organisation may in
    turn limit the wage gains which might otherwise result from
    increases in productivity, or may exclude low paying industries
    from forces of wage leadership (as might the small firm
    competitive market environment). In demonstrating that
    characteristics are related to causes in this complex manner,
    the analysis has implied that it is of little explanatory value,
    and possibly misleading, to attempt to isolate and measure the
    impact of one or a particular combination of shared
    characteristics (e.g. 'industrial' factors) and to compare their
    contribution with that of others (e.g. 'individual'/occupational
    factors).

2. Factors peculiar to low paying manufacturing industries
    Inadequate demand conditions in both product and labour markets
    appear to be additional factors of importance in accounting for
    low earnings in low paying manufacturing industries. These
    conditions reflect the unfavourable influence of a number of
    structural changes and developments in the British economy which
    have occurred in response to the rising price of raw material
    imports, rising incomes and changing tastes in the home market,
    and more recently in response to the intensification of inter-
    national competition. The below average proportions of unskilled
    manual employees in low paying manufacturing industries
    challenge the general validity of both human capital theories of
    wage determination and the Bosanquet-Doeringer-Piore model of
    labour market duality.

3. Factors peculiar to low paying service industries The
    characteristics of low paying service industries on the other
    hand largely accord with those of a secondary labour market as
    depicted in the Doeringer-Piore model. From this perspective,
    market duality and low pay reflect the barriers to labour
    mobility arising from the manpower policies adopted by employers
    in the primary sector. The model has been criticised by Rubery
    who substitutes trade unions for employers as the main agents
    giving rise to labour immobility and through which segmented

labour markets are developed. Both models imply, however, that
the prevalence of low pay in the service sector derives
ultimately from the labour-intensive 'nature' of these industries
and from their relative exclusion from advances in technology and
the general trend towards increasing concentration of economic
activity.

Post-war trends in employment in the service sector have also
contributed to low pay. In the public services, low pay may
partly reflect government attempts to restrict the growth of
public expenditure, given the labour-intensive 'non-productive'
nature of the greater part of public employment. In the service
sector generally, wages appear to have been depressed through
'oversupply'. Rubery suggests that the response of trade unions
to recent changes in the distribution and composition of
employment has exacerbated competitive conditions for service
workers. For Braverman, the influence of these structural
changes on both supply and demand conditions in service labour
markets represents a natural tendency in capitalist economies
toward the pauperization of the mass of workers. Certainly, the
changes which have occurred have at least contributed to the
persistence of low average earnings in service industries and at
the same time have enlarged the share in employment of service
industries relative to that of other sectors of the economy. The
net effect has been to alter the 'typicality' of the low paid
employee over the post-war period.

Finally, the methods of wage payment characterising service
industries and in particular the low reliance on PBR systems of
payment may have additionally contributed to low earnings.
Workers are afforded relatively few opportunities to boost their
earnings above basic pay and are offered little incentive to
improve productivity or efficiency. In addition the 'wage spiral
effect' resulting from the frequent disturbance of piece-rate/
time-rate differentials is less likely to occur. Again, however,
the low reliance on PBR schemes in the service sector may itself
be considered a function of technology or developments in
economic structure.

4. <u>General</u> A strong general theme throughout the discussion in
Sections 2 and 3 has been the extent to which the causes of low
pay are endogenous to the economic system.

THE POST-WAR TRADE UNION RESPONSE

1. THE POST-WAR RESPONSE : 1945-78

An examination of annual TUC Reports since 1945 suggests that trade
union concern over low pay, as a distinct wage policy issue, is a
comparatively recent development in British post-war industrial
relations. The Reports show that prior to the mid-1960s, the topic was
rarely raised in the General Council's written submissions to Congress
or in the debates which followed. Not until the latter half of the
1960s did 'low pay' appear to feature as a regular and prominent issue
for debate. This pattern may best be understood following an account
of the major developments in trade union wage policy over the post-
war period. The discussion which follows considers union policy
primarily at the level of the TUC, with special reference to those
developments relating to low pay, and with particular focus on the
interaction of government and TUC wages policies since 1945. Some
reasons are then suggested for the apparent initial lack, and
subsequent enhancement, of trade union interest in the topic.

A. 1945-51

Between 1945-51, the TUC co-operated closely with the newly-elected
Labour Government. Indeed, Hobsbawm describes this period as one in
which 'trade unions were so tightly enmeshed in the web of big
business and government that so traditional an activity as the strike
became, at most times, associated almost entirely with unofficial
action or rank-and-file revolt'. (1) The twin preoccupation of both
TUC and Government in this period appeared to be that of restricting
wage increases, while increasing productivity, as part of the post-war
recovery programme. This policy was aimed at countering the
inflationary pressures generated during the war years, and a resultant
balance-of-payments crisis, a crisis exacerbated by the sudden
termination of American 'lend-lease' assistance in Autumn 1945. Prices
had to be reduced and productivity increased if the export drive,
crucial to national recovery, was to succeed.
   In the immediate post-war years (1945-47) the question of low pay
did not appear to be raised in the TUC's dealings with Government.
Activity appeared to be focussed chiefly on laws relating to strikes,

and the twin issues of productivity and wage restraint. For example, in 1945, the Minister of Labour persuaded the General Council to agree to the continuation of 'Order 1305' of the Emergency Powers (Defence) Act which made all strikes illegal until it was withdrawn in 1951. In 1946, Ernest Bevin met with the TUC to emphasise the importance of increased production; and the General Council responded by nominating a number of its own members to the National Production Advisory Council on industry, under the Chairmanship of the Board of Trade.

In 1947, the Government's increasing anxiety over the economic situation led it to issue a White Paper calling for co-operation from the General Council in combating inflation, balancing foreign trade and in increasing the labour force in vital undermanned industries. (2) The General Council again readily responded by urging the re-constitution of joint production committees in factories (which had mostly faded away after the War), and by undertaking to examine the possibility of itself recommending a measure of wage restraint to member unions. Only one condition for co-operation was stated: that 'Nothing in the White Paper was to be taken as restricting the rights of the Unions to make claims through the normal collective bargaining arrangements. Such claims should be treated on their own merits'. (3) Priority for the low paid, however, was not stipulated as a condition of co-operation.

The first TUC reference to low pay in the context of wage policy was in response to a further White Paper issued in 1948 which called for more vigorous (but still voluntary) wage restraint. The document stated that there was 'no justification at the present time for any rise in incomes from profits, rent, or other like sources and that rises in wages or salaries should only be asked for and agreed upon in the exceptional cases mentioned above'. (4) The 'exceptional cases' were specified in very general terms as those 'in which increases in wages and salaries would be justified from a national point of view'. (5) Only the case of undermanned industries was cited as an example.

The White Paper was discussed shortly after at a conference of trade union executives called by the General Council. By a substantial majority, the conference agreed that its provisions relating to wage restraint were acceptable, providing that three further grounds for exceptional wage increases were recognised. The principles of the White Paper had to:

(i)   'admit the justification for claims for increased wages where these increases are based upon the fact of increased output';

(ii)   'admit the necessity of adjusting the wages of workers whose incomes are below a reasonable standard of subsistence';

(iii)   'recognise the need to safeguard those wage differentials which are an essential element in the wages structure of many important industries, and are required to sustain those standards of craftsmanship, training and experience that contribute directly to industrial efficiency and higher productivity'. (6)

A policy of restraint, incorporating both special priority for the
low paid and provisions for maintaining wage differentials, might
seem somewhat contradictory or self-defeating. Indeed, Flanders
argued that taken severally, and without further definition, the TUC's
conditions provided grounds enough for most trade unions to argue that
satisfaction of their claim was in the national interest. (7) Little
priority, however, appears to have been attached to the conditions in
subsequent developments. The Government gave no indication of what it
thought of the TUC's interpretation of its policy, while the TUC,
though pledged only to restrict wage claims to those which were
compatible with the terms of its own declaration, in practice went
much further. Flanders notes that the TUC attempted - and with
considerable success - to hold back all wage claims on the grounds of
the country's economic difficulties. Hence, the index of full-time
weekly wage rates which had risen by six points in the year preceding
June 1948 gained but another four during the following two years.
Little account was taken of the low pay criterion: 'From time to time
there were references by Government spokesmen and trade union leaders
to the justification of wage increases for lower paid workers but
even this one objective remained undefined.' (8)

By 1949, the General Council was experiencing difficulties in
maintaining its support for the Government. These were increased by
the development of a formidable Communist opposition in key positions
within a number of prominent unions. Communist opposition to the
Government's policies did not appear, however, to rest on any
particular concern for the lower paid, but mainly reflected the
British Communist Party's decision in 1947 to boycott the European
Recovery Programme and any collaboration likely to aid the production
drive. Indeed, Pelling argues that the main opponents of wage
restraint were those unions (both Communist and non-Communist
dominated) representing skilled manual workers whose members resented
the decline in their differential advantage over the unskilled - a
process which had then been going on for some time. (9) This implies
that it was non-adherence to the differential criterion rather than
to the low pay criterion of the TUC's declaration which provoked most
opposition to wage restraint during this period.

This is further suggested by evidence gathered by Runciman. In
contrasting the criteria underlying wage claims and disputes in the
pre-war period with those of the immediate post-war period, a marked
shift in emphasis was noticed from claims resting on notions of
subsistence, or for greater equality in earnings, to those based on
arguments for the maintenance of differentials:

'There is certainly a notable change between the inter-war
and post-war periods. In the inter-war period, the greater
number of disputes were about either the level below which
wages would not be regarded as providing subsistence, or the
changes made possible (or necessary) by the economic
situation of the particular firm or industry concerned.
After 1945, the achievement of full employment, and the
governmental policy of wage restraint which was in part a
result of it, changed the language and assumptions within
which wage disputes were conducted. Appeals to justice came

more often to be based on differentials ... But ... the
wage claims made seldom rested on any broad principle of
egalitarianism'. (10)

In the event, however, the policy of restrain broke down through
external economic pressures. The devaluation of sterling in late 1949
had caused a sharp rise in the prices of sterling imports, and this
was strongly reinforced by the increase in world market prices brought
about by the Korean War. Flanders points out, however, that the TUC
still attempted to encourage wage restraint and recommended a virtual
wages standstill until the end of 1950. In the light of the rapid
price rises, however, this policy was rejected by member unions. A
subsequent modified recommendation for restraint, incorporating a
clause calling for 'greater flexibility of wage movements in the
future' (though no mention of low pay) was also rejected. Hence, from
the start of 1950 until October 1951 when Labour lost office, the
policy of restraint was largely abandoned.

B.   1951-64

Pelling observes that the TUC was initially prepared to co-operate
with the newly-elected Conservative Government:

> 'For their part, the TUC leaders, led by Deakin of the
> Transport and General, Tom Williamson of the General and
> Municipal and Will Lawther of the mineworkers, saw to it that
> the cautious and moderate policy which they had pursued under
> the Labour Government was maintained under the Conservatives.
> Among other things, they ensured that resolutions denouncing
> all forms of wage restraint - such as were regularly
> submitted to Congress by the Communist-dominated unions -
> were voted down by adequate majorities'. (11)

The new Government first relied on fiscal and monetary measures to
curb inflation. It was not long, however, before the Chancellor
presented a statement to a meeting of the National Joint Advisory
Council to the Minister of Labour in May 1952 in which he suggested
that a committee should be appointed to examine 'the possibility of
devising methods of relating wages more closely to productivity and of
modifying the existing wage structures of many of our industries with
this end in view'. (12) However, this proposal failed to win the
support of the TUC. Pelling argues that the TUC's non-co-operation
mainly reflected a feeling among unionists that the Government's
recent fiscal and monetary policies - reducing food subsidies, and
giving relief in direct taxation, for example - had impaired their
living standards. There was also a strong feeling that enough
sacrifice had been made in the cause of post-war reconstruction, given
the improved economic climate of the early 1950s. (13)

Flanders argues that in failing to gain union support for some
measure of wage restraint by overt means, the Government then adopted
'more devious methods'. For example, a number of important wage claims
were being wholly rejected by arbitration tribunals. This coincided
with an apparent stiffening of employers' resistance in negotiations

so that more claims were being referred to arbitration. During 1953, the awards of the Industrial Disputes Tribunal were so small and so similar 'that trade unionists accused it of following a wages policy'. (14)

A further example of this more covert approach was the decision by the Minister of Labour to refer back for reconsideration the proposals for wage increases submitted by twelve wages councils in 1952. The TUC Economic Committee responded by demanding an urgent meeting with the Prime Minister. It is significant to note, however, that the protest lodged with the Prime Minister was not expressed in terms of concern for a section of the lowest paid workers whose wage increases had been squashed. Rather, Pelling argues that the protest was against Government intrusion 'into the normal processes of wage determination'. Hence, the Minister of Labour was obliged to disavow any intention of 'interfering with any of the functions of Wages Councils, including that of submitting proposals for fixing the remuneration of workers or of undermining their authority'. (15)

Indeed, little concern for the low paid was apparent in wage claims submitted during this period, and the sort of change which Runciman described appeared to become more pronounced. For example, Flanders observes that in the first half of the 1950s there was a strong shift in preference from flat-rate to percentage increases: 'The previously well established trend towards a narrowing of the percentage skill differential was checked. Disputes over wage differentials became more frequent'. (16) This is consistent with the NBPI evidence cited in Chapter 2 which showed a narrowing of differentials between skilled and unskilled manual workers up to 1950 followed by a widening between 1950 and 1960.

Possibly on account of the more covert methods chosen by the Government in applying wage restraint in the initial half of the 1950s, the TUC largely boycotted further Government initiatives. It refused to co-operate, for example, in the policy introduced in May 1956 for the establishment of a 'Price Plateau'. This involved assurances from the nationalised industries and private employers' organisations that they would not increase prices, and in effect, the policy meant that wage restraint was to be imposed by employers at the calculated risk of endangering industrial peace. The main outcome was the prolonged shipbuilding and engineering strikes of 1957. The TUC similarly refused to co-operate with the Council on Prices, Productivity and Incomes set up in 1957, an advisory body charged with keeping under review changes in prices, incomes and productivity so as to provide an analytical framework for the Government's economic policies. Nor was TUC support forthcoming for the 'Pay Pause' - a temporary halt to any increases in wages, salaries and dividends introduced in July 1961 - and the Government was forced to use its influence over public sector pay settlements to make the policy effective. In none of the White Papers or Chancellors' Statements introducing these policies was there any mention of preferential treatment for the low paid. Indeed, few other circumstances were specified where exceptional treatment might be justified.

When the period set for the pay pause was coming to an end, the TUC also declined the Government's invitation to help it work out a more permanent machinery for the application of an incomes policy.

Undeterred, the Government issued a White Paper proposing a 'Guiding Light' for annual increases in wages and salaries of between 2-2½%. The only specified exception to this norm was where 'those concerned made a direct contribution, by accepting more exacting work, or more onerous conditions, or by a renunciation of restrictive practices, to an increase of productivity and a reduction of costs'. (17)

In pursuing its policy of promoting a more permanent form of incomes policy, the Government then set up the National Incomes Commission (NIC) in the latter half of 1962, a body intended as an agency of long-term economic planning. In considering the justification for pay settlements which would be referred to it, the NIC was required, in its terms of reference, to have regard to a wider range of criteria than had hitherto been specified in previous White Papers. The principle that wage increases should not outstrip productivity growth was maintained, but in addition, the Commission was to have regard to: the manpower needs of the industry concerned; prices, profit margins, dividends and efficiency considerations; the possible differential repercussions of settlements; and, though not specifically referring to low pay, regard to 'the desirability of paying a fair reward for the work done'. (18) However, the TUC again failed to support the Commission, largely on the ground that 'it was based on a wrong assumption - that general restraint was needed as part of an anti-inflationary policy. The facts did not and could not be made to sustain an argument that Britain was drifting into an inflationary situation'. (19) In consequence, the 'fair reward' clause was not further developed nor defined. The NIC did not, in any case, have much influence on the level of actual settlements, and was dissolved when the Conservatives lost office in 1964.

C. 1964-78

Flanders describes the period following the election of the new Labour Government as one in which incomes policy entered a 'new phase'. He was referring to an apparent change in the professed role of incomes policy which occurred in this period from that of a 'euphemism for wage restraint' or an 'improvised response to the latest balance-of-payments crisis' to a 'central instrument of economic planning'. (20) Hyman and Brough note a similar shift in emphasis. From 1964, incomes policy came to be viewed as a 'positive weapon of reform' as opposed to a 'negative mechanism of restraint'. Ethical arguments were increasingly incorporated into policies and the notion of incomes policy as an instrument of social justice gained currency. (21) Some indication of this change was in evidence in the later policies of the previous Conservative administration, for example, the 'fair reward' clause in the terms of reference of the NIC. It is from this new phase that the topic of low pay first appears to have emerged, gained impetus and remained as a distinct issue of prominence in the policies of both trade unions and governments.

On the Government's part, the first official endorsement of the perspective was in the drawing up of a 'Joint Statement of Intent' which was later signed by representatives of the Government, employers' organisations and the TUC in December 1964. This pledged all three parties to co-operate with proposed Government machinery for regulating prices and incomes. The statement opened by stressing that 'the Government's ... social objective is to ensure that the benefits of faster growth are distributed in a way that satisfies the claims of social need and justice'. (22) The terms of the declaration were defined shortly after in two White Papers. The first set out the proposed machinery. The NBPI would be created to replace the NIC and deal with the application of policy to particular cases. A second White Paper issued in April 1965 set out the criteria for judging individual price changes and pay settlements, and it was in this document that the topic of low pay was first raised by a government in the context of incomes policy. A norm of $3-3\frac{1}{2}\%$ was set for the annual rate of increase in average earnings. This limit was felt to be necessary to achieve the 4% rate of economic growth envisaged in the National Plan, the economic plan for expansion framed by George Brown in 1964. However, four acceptable grounds for exceptional wage increases above the norm were specified. Of these, three closely paralleled the proposals of the previous Conservative Government and related to productivity, undermanning and comparability considerations. A fourth, however, was 'where there is general recognition that existing wage and salary levels are too low to maintain a reasonable standard of living'. (23)

Priority for the low paid was largely maintained in subsequent formulations of the policy. The only exception was during the six month 'freeze' on earnings from July 1966 imposed through the Prices and Incomes Act 1966. This was in response to a run on sterling and a resultant balance-of-payments crisis, a crisis which led to the abandonment of the National Plan. The freeze applied to virtually all earnings, including those of the low paid, one of the few exceptions being made for increases in pay resulting from increased productivity. However, in the period of 'severe restraint' which followed between January and June 1967, the low paid were again accorded special exemption from a statutory nil norm: 'Improvement of the standard of living of the worst off members of the community is a primary social objective ... However, it will be necessary to ensure that any increases justified on these grounds are confined to the lowest paid workers and not to other workers'. (24) The low pay exception clause of the April 1965 White Paper cited above was reintroduced during the statutory $3-3\frac{1}{2}\%$ norm imposed between July 1967 and March 1968, and continued to apply during the statutory $3\frac{1}{2}\%$ 'ceiling' between April 1968 and December 1969 and the $2\frac{1}{2}-4\frac{1}{2}\%$ non-statutory guideline for pay increases in operation between January and June 1970. Under these policies, numerous claims for special treatment on the ground of low pay were referred to the NBPI, and the many 'low pay reference' (and other) Reports issued by the Board in the latter half of the 1960s bear further witness to the topicality of the issue in public policy during this period. (25)

The promotion of social justice and preferential treatment for the low paid were also presented as objectives of policies operated by the Heath Government between 1970 and 1974. For its first two years of office, the Government did not operate a formal incomes policy. However, concern for the consequences of low pay was implied by the introduction of FIS in August 1971, payable to low income families whose breadwinner was in full-time employment.

In 1972, a 90-day freeze was introduced to combat a resurgence of economic difficulties and a further balance-of-payments crisis. The low paid were not exempt. However, the Government justified the statutory Stage 2 policy of £1 + 4% which followed in April 1973 as 'designed to favour low paid workers for whom it would give a better deal than a percentage limit'. (26) Stage 3 introduced in October 1973 also potentially favoured the low paid. This imposed limits on settlements of £2.25 per week or 7% (whichever was larger) and introduced flat-rate threshold payments to compensate for rises in the cost of living. Trinder estimates that this formula permitted increases of up to 21.8% per annum for workers on £25 per week in October 1973 (then two-thirds of average male manual earnings) as compared with 12.6% for 'Affluent Workers' on £57 per week (one and a half times average male manual earnings in October 1973). (27)

The 'Social Contract', as its title implies, was perhaps the most explicit official endorsement of the broader conception of incomes policy as an agent of social and economic planning and reform. The terms of the Contract were drawn up at various TUC-Labour Party Liaison Committee meetings held in late 1973 and were developed and implemented after Labour had gained power in February 1974. The basis of the Contract was an undertaking by Government to carry out various economic, social and legislative reforms (many of which fell outside the immediate sphere of collective bargaining), in return for which the TUC would encourage memeber unions to apply a measure of wage restraint. Measures proposed on the Government side included: the repeal of the Conservative Government's Industrial Relations Act; an end to statutory pay controls; increases in old age pensions; subsidies to essential food items; greater control of prices; a freeze on rents; and holding down mortgage rates.

For its part, the TUC issued Guidelines to negotiators which recommended that the level of pay settlements over the following 12 months should not exceed that which compensated for the rise in the cost of living. A 12 month gap between major settlements was also to be observed. Once again, however, special treatment for the low paid was an agreed objective of the policy. A further recommendation of the TUC Guidelines (as endorsed by Government) was that 'Priority should also be given to attaining reasonable minimum standards, including the TUC's low pay target of a £25 minimum basic rate with higher minimum earnings, for a normal working week for those aged 18 and over'. (28) The £25 figure was later raised to £30 at the 1974 September TUC.

Priority for the low paid was implied in subsequent voluntary pay formulae agreed between the Government and the TUC within the frame-work of the Contract. The Stage I formula introduced in August 1975 specified a flat-rate £6 limit on annual increases for those earning less than £8,500 per year, with no increases for those earning more. Stage II which followed in July 1976 specified maximum annual increases of £2.50 per week on earnings up to £50 per week, 5% on earnings of £50.80 per week and £4 on earnings of £80 or more per week. Both formulae thus potentially favoured the low paid by providing for relatively higher percentage increases for those on low earnings.

Stage III, introduced in July 1977, proposed a general level of pay settlements moderate enough to ensure that the national annual earnings increase was no more than 10%. Though the low paid were not

specifically exempted from this guidline, the 'kitty principle' outlined in the White Paper introducing the policy allowed negotiators
flexibility to structure settlements in whatever way best suited their
circumstances, so long as 'the total settlement' was kept in single
figures. (29) Specific reference to the low paid returned in the final
Stage IV of the policy introduced in a White Paper in July 1978. This
specified a guideline of 5% for pay settlements in the year to follow.
To help the lowest paid, however, 'the Government would be ready to
see higher percentage increases where the resulting earnings were no
more than £44.50 for a normal full-time week. This level of earnings
represents the TUC minimum pay target of £30 in 1974-75 updated by the
maximum increases generally available under subsequent policies
including those set out in this White Paper'. (30)

The trade union response throughout this period is considered in
greater detail in Chapter 6. It may be noted, however, that in
contrast to 1948, when the low pay issue was raised by the TUC in the
context of discussions on incomes policy, the incorporation of low pay
provisions in the policies described above did not appear, initially
at least, to derive from trade union pressure:

'Thus, when the crucial formative debates on incomes and wages
were taking place within the trade union and Labour Movement
in 1963 there was little recognition of the vital need to
build into the general policies a specific element designed
to solve the particular problem of the low paid section of the
working class. Instead there was a general acceptance that the
entire problem was to manage the economic policy of a society
in the stage of scientific revolution in such a way that it
would maximize the employment of productive resources and
that wages would increase in proportion to rising productivity
while unemployment was eliminated and prices stabilized. In
this way the resulting 'planned growth of incomes' would
produce a corresponding rise in living standards including,
presumably, those of the low paid'. (31)

Following the Government's initiative, however, trade union interest
in the issue began to mount. The first important discussions on the
topic seem to have been those which took place at the annual TUC
Congress in September 1966, in relation to a debate on whether the TUC
should continue to support the Government's incomes policy. At that
time, trade unionists were divided in their attitudes towards the 'new
phase' of policies. Several unions, including the influential Transport
and General Workers' Union, were strongly opposed to any form of wage
restraint, and opposition stiffened following the introduction of the
statutory freeze in July 1966. Discussion on low pay was occasioned by
the General Council's Report to Congress which, in attempting to
canvass support for the Government, emphasised that Government policy
'must take account of the need to promote social equity, and in
particular to protect groups of very low paid workers'. (32) A motion
reaffirming this theme was moved by Sir William Carron (AUEW) which,
while supporting the General Council's 'reluctant acquiescence' to the
freeze, also demanded 'effective measures to assist lower paid workers,
particularly those whose earnings are close to modern conceptions of

subsistence levels', and requested that the General Council investigate ways and means of tackling the problem. (33) The motion was seconded by Lord Cooper (GMWU), and in the debate which followed, the low pay issue was a frequent theme in arguments both for and against further co-operation with the Government. For example, delegates from COHSE (health), EEPTU (electricians) and the NUM referred to the detrimental effect of a 'free-for-all' on the low paid as an important reason for maintaining support, while the opposite position was taken by Alan Fisher of NUPE, who argued against further co-operation mainly on the ground that the low paid were not to be exempted from the freeze. The mood of the Congress was perhaps best summarised in the voting, where a resolution in support of the General Council's Report was carried by a mere 344,000 votes, while William Carron's motion which supported the Report but also expressed concern for the low paid, was carried by a substantial majority of 1,122,000 votes, a result implying that further union co-operation would be conditional upon the incorporation of measures to assist the low paid into future policies.

Following the 1966 Congress, trade union concern over low pay gathered momentum. An examination of subsequent TUC Reports shows that the topic continued to be raised with regularity in discussions on incomes policies, and particularly common were resolutions denouncing the failure of successive stages of policy to deal adequately with the problem. The topic also began to be raised outside the context of discussions on incomes policy and appeared to develop from 1966 as a distinct wages policy issue in itself.

The TUC's commitment to minimum wage targets from 1967 provides one indication of the mounting concern. The first minimum target of £15 per week for a normal 40 hour week was adopted in principle at the 1967 Congress following a resolution moved by Frank Cousins (TGWU). Congress resolved that this was the minimum earnings figure at which negotiators should aim and pledged support for unions involved in disputes to achieve this target. A further resolution by Jack Jones at the 1969 Congress raised the minimum to £16.50. At the 1971 Congress, this figure was increased to £20 following a resolution by Harry Urwin, again of the TGWU. A resolution by Bernard Dix (NUPE) raised the target to £25 at the 1973 Congress, and, as noted earlier, this figure was subsequently raised to £30 at the 1974 Congress, following a resolution moved by David Basnett of the GMWU. (34)

A second indicator is the extent to which the low pay issue has become an important bargaining and propaganda weapon in a number of recent wage claims and disputes, particularly in the public sector. For example, Cliff refers to 'the revolt of the low paid' in 1970 when local authority manual workers went on strike, and again in 1974 when hospital ancillary staff and civil servants took industrial action for the first time. (35) Public sector disputes during the 1979 'winter of discontent' were also fought on the low pay platform.

At the level of the TUC, the first policies and proposals for tackling low pay were set out in the first of the TUC's annual Economic Reviews published in January 1968. (36) Policies considered included: the establishment of a £15 minimum earnings guarantee for a 40 hour week; improving productivity and efficiency in low paying sectors; and the establishment of a statutory national minimum wage.

These proposals were reiterated in the 1969 Economic Review where, in addition, certain changes to the tax and social security systems were recommended. Policies for tackling low pay (or the related problem of family poverty) were discussed in almost all subsequent Reviews published throughout the 1970s.

The first TUC policy document to be devoted entirely to low pay was the Report of a working party of TUC staff and trade union research officers set up in 1969 to review the whole problem area and come up with proposals for its solution. The Report was published in 1970. (37) The introduction of a statutory national minimum wage, improvements to productivity and efficiency and reforms in the taxation and social security systems were again discussed as possible solutions. Ways in which the collective bargaining process could be modified to assist the low paid were also discussed. The first of the TUC's series of 'Reviews of Collective Bargaining Developments' published in 1972 was also largely devoted to the topic. (38) In addition, in the late 1960s - early 1970s, the General Council initiated a series of discussions with unions organising in low paying sectors and directed particular attention to the limitations which wages councils imposed on efforts to eradicate low pay. Finally, as noted earlier, policies to eliminate low pay remained a central theme in TUC discussions with Government in developing the terms of the Social Contract.

2.   REASONS FOR EMERGENCE OF TRADE UNION CONCERN

The discussion has shown that trade union concern over low pay has emerged when governments - especially Labour Governments - have sought to gain union support for policies of wage restraint - that is, briefly in 1948, and again in the mid-1960s. Throughout the 1950s, on the other hand, when union-government relations were less cordial (possibly on account of the more covert approach to wage restraint adopted by the Conservative Government), the issue did not appear to arise. This pattern suggests that the low pay issue comes to the forefront in trade union and public policy when being employed as a form of concession in making the idea of wage restraint seem more acceptable or palatable to trade unionists, at least in times when union-government relations are in other respects relatively harmonious. Though in 1948, the issue was raised by the TUC rather than the Government, this interpretation remains plausible, given the TUC's commitment to Government policies at that time and the apparent isolation of the General Council from the rank and file in this respect. (39)

This sort of explanation finds favour with Hyman and Brough who extend it to suggest that the injection of notions of equity and fairness and of low pay provisions into recent incomes policies was part of some deceitful ploy instituted by governments with the sole aim of achieving wage restraint. Referring to lack of progress made in the 1960s in dealing with low pay, the authors comment:

'The implication would seem to be that - however sincere may be some advocates of incomes policy as an instrument of reformative justice - the rhetoric of equity is employed within public policy as a more or less cynical attempt to achieve worker and

trade union support for restrictions on their bargaining
activities. In this respect, notions of fairness and
social justice are used for unashamedly ideological
purposes'. (40)

However, given the way in which low pay has developed and remained
since the mid-1960s as a trade union policy issue of some prominence,
this interpretation provides, at most, a partial explanation.

The recent emergence of trade union concern may be further related
to changes in the political composition of the TUC over the post-war
period, in particular, the succession of Frank Cousins from Deakin,
and the later election of Jack Jones to the leadership of the TGWU;
and the accession of Hugh Scanlon to the leadership of the AUEW.
Leaders like Jones and Scanlon who were elected on left-wing
platforms (and described by Pelling as 'militants') are likely to
have been more sympathetic to redistributive and other measures
designed to favour the low paid and may have influenced TUC policy to
this effect.

A third reason may relate to the erosion during the 1960s of a
belief current in the Macmillan 'never-had-it-so-good' era that
poverty in Britain had been eliminated. This view, briefly mentioned
in Chapter 2, was apparently widely accepted and may have influenced
trade union policy during the 1950s. Coates and Silburn comment:

'During the fifties, the myth that widespread material poverty
had been finally and triumphantly overcome was so universally
current, so widely accepted by politicians, social commentators
and the general public alike, that for a decade or more public
controversy and political discussion were engrossed by the new
(and fundamentally more encouraging) problem of what people
are still pleased to call the 'Affluent Society'. The period
since the end of the Second World War was interpreted as one
of more or less uninterrupted and continuing economic growth,
with the new wealth being distributed increasingly equitably
throughout the population. The age-old malaise of poverty, far
from being an endemic problem facing a mass of the population,
was felt to be a slight social hangover, a problem affecting
tiny groups of people who, through their incompetence or
fecklessness, were failing to share in the new affluence'. (41)

The authors suggest that this myth arose from the striking contrast
of material well-being between the 1930s and 1950s; 'To those whose
reflexes had been conditioned during the lean years of the Depression,
the widespread prosperity of the fifties was quite undeniable'. (42)

As was noted in Chapter 2, Abel-Smith and Townsend, in 1965, were
among the first to challenge the view. The work of Professor Titmuss
was also particularly influential. (43) Moreover, poverty was 're-
discovered' in a number of Government surveys conducted in the latter
half of the 1960s. The findings of studies such as these may have
contributed to the growing awareness within the trade union movement
of the problems of poverty and low pay. Indeed, it was in response to
the findings of the Government's 1966 'Circumstances of Families'
report (44) that a resolution was moved (for the first time in many

years) at the 1967 TUC Congress calling for 'the abolition of poverty'. (45)

The amount of attention devoted in recent TUC policy documents to the poverty trap, as discussed in Chapter 2, suggests that this was a fourth factor involved. The effects of the trap were first noticeable in the late 1960s and became more apparent during the 1970s. This reflected the joint effects of a progressive fall in the tax threshold over the post-war period, together with the extension, in the late 1960s - early 1970s, of means-tested benefits to those in full-time employment (especially FIS introduced in August 1971). Table 5.1 expresses the fall in the tax threshold from 1959/60 as a proportion of average male earnings for a single man, and for a married man with two and four children respectively. The Table shows that for the tax year 1959/60 only some 20% of the earnings of a married man on average earnings and with two children was taxable, whereas in 1975/76, the corresponding proportion had risen to over 55%. Pond et al attribute these figures to the failure of governments to raise thresholds sufficiently to compensate for the large increases in money earnings which accompanied the rapid inflation of the 1960s and 1970s. (46)

TABLE 5.1   Tax Threshold as a Percentage of Average Male Earnings* : 1960-76

Tax Year	Single man	Married man with 2 children (aged Under 11)	Married man with 4 children (aged Under 11)
1959-60	27.4	79.2	108.3
1964-65	30.3	75.9	101.8
1970-71	28.6	54.3	60.1
1972-73	31.8	57.4	67.4
1973-74	28.0	52.4	65.6
1974-75	24.7	57.1	66.0
1975-76	21.8	44.6	56.8

* Average weekly earnings of men, aged 21 and over, in October of each year.

Source: C. Pond, F. Field and S. Winyard, Trade Unions and Taxation, Studies for Trade Unionists, Vol.2, No.6, Workers Educational Association, June 1976, Table 3, p. 4.

The TUC itself attributed growing concern over low pay in the 1960s to 'subjective feelings' on the part of many workers 'that they have been left behind at a time when living standards generally have been rising'. (47) It was argued, however, that there was little evidence that earnings at the bottom had moved further from the average and that such feelings arose 'from greater awareness, through mass media, of the extent to which many groups are receiving very large pay packets'. (48) Data limitations make it difficult to confirm this interpretation. However, for male manual employees at least, the figures in Table 2.4 of Chapter 2 show that the low paid did lose some ground between 1960 and 1970, though the change was very small. The lowest decile, expressed as a percentage of median earnings was 70.6% in 1960 as compared with 67.3% in 1970.

Nevertheless, the belief that the dispersion of earnings had widened over this period was fairly widespread and one apparently shared by the Government. For example, in a 1969 White Paper, the Government invited unions and employers to join with it in working out 'solutions to the problem of those low paid workers who had been unjustifiably left behind in the scramble of wage bargaining'. (49) Cliff also shared this belief and argued that the 'revolt of the low paid' in 1970, and indeed the wages and strike 'explosion' of 1969-70 were, in part, consequences of the emphasis in incomes policies of the 1960s on increased productivity as the main criterion for exceptional wage increases. The growth of productivity bargaining meant that the earnings of the low paid, who predominantly comprised workers who could not easily make productivity concessions, fell relatively to the earnings of other groups of workers. (50)

3.   SUMMARY AND CONCLUSIONS

Only relatively recently has the low pay problem occupied a position of some prominence in British post-war industrial relations. Prior to the mid-1960s, little concern for the low paid was apparent in the wages policies pursued by governments or the TUC. Nor did it seem to be a pertinent issue underlying wage claims or disputes. The trade union response to the problem has been influenced by the differing approaches of governments towards incomes policy. The emergence of trade union concern followed the 'new phase' of policies introduced during the 1960s. The incorporation of low pay provisions into policies adopted since 1964 appears to have been aimed at gaining trade union co-operation in wage restraint, an approach which has led some to doubt the sincerity of recent public policy relating to low pay. Government initiatives in the area of incomes policy do not fully account for the way in which the low pay problem has developed and remained as a distinct and prominent trade union policy issue. Additional factors involved relate to: changes in the political composition of the TUC over the post-war period; the 'rediscovery' of poverty during the 1960s; the increasing influence of the poverty-trap in the late 1960s - early 1970s; and to the real or imagined impact of incomes policies operated during the 1960s on the relative earnings position of the low paid.

1. THE OBJECTIVES OF POLICY

Two main conceptions of low pay are apparent from recent trade union policy documents on the issue: low pay as a problem of family poverty; and as a problem of earnings or income inequality. Most often, however, it is argued that the main problem ought to be viewed as one of poverty. For example, writing in 1968, Edmonds and Radice (GMWU) distinguished 'relative low pay' from 'absolute low pay' and argued that policy should primarily be directed towards eliminating the latter:

'In our opinion, a policy to improve low pay must begin with a distinction between unjust wage relativities which affect all workers and the much more serious problem of pay which is so low in absolute terms that it causes, or may cause hardship or deprivation. We have to pinpoint an income level which society considers to be a reasonable minimum and assess the pay of workers in relation to that'. (1)

Fisher and Dix (NUPE) drew a similar distinction in 1974 and again assigned primary importance to a 'poverty' definition:

'A more careful consideration will show that ... (views on low pay) ... tend to fall into two distinct major categories ... The first is concerned with establishing a relative standard of living, the second is concerned with meeting basic standards. One is primarily concerned with desires encouraged by prospects of affluence while the other is concerned with needs directed by the fear of poverty. At this point in time we are convinced that attention must be concentrated on the second category, and that any policy for the elimination of low pay must establish as its foundation a defined level of basic pay sufficient to provide an acceptable basic standard of living'. (2)

TUC discussion documents on the topic also seem to imply the existence of some 'basic' or 'acceptable' minimum standard of living and that the promotion of the real incomes of low earners and their families to this level would largely solve the problem irrespective of any major change to the distribution of earnings. Admittedly, in deriving numerical definitions of low pay the TUC has employed relative criteria similar to those discussed in Chapter 2, (3) and indeed, policy has primarily been directed to securing relative improvements (albeit modest) to the earnings position of the lower paid. However, this approach is most often justified on <u>economic</u> considerations rather than grounds of equity, a common argument being that increases for the lower paid, if reflected proportionately throughout the wages structure, would have serious inflationary consequences which would have a disproportionate impact on the living standards of the low paid - and hence fail to raise their real income to the desired <u>minimum</u> level. (4) These considerations apart, however, a reduction in the spread of earnings <u>per se</u> is rarely presented as a prerequisite to solving low pay.

This conceptual separation of the low pay issue from the more general problem of economic inequality is, of course, open to criticism. As was pointed out in Chapter 2, poverty itself may be viewed as a relative concept. Indeed, Runciman has argued that there can be no logical definition of absolute poverty:

> 'There are, perhaps, 'absolute' needs in the sense of what is required by the human organism in order to survive. But they do not furnish a useful definition of 'absolute', either in the sense of not relative or in the sense of universally valid. The level of so-called absolute need can be just as well fixed at one level as another. It may be that progressively more extravagant wants come to be felt as needs because progressively higher comparisons become plausible; but there is no necessary reason why a sense of need deriving from an external reference group should be any less 'absolute' or less valid. Why is education, say, a less 'absolute' need than an adequate diet?' (5)

The apparent reluctance on the part of union policy-makers to view the problem in relative terms possibly reflects the difficulty of formulating unified and agreed policies on low pay which are acceptable to unions with differing, and possibly opposing, objectives. Clearly, some union leaders, especially those representing large groups of lower paid workers, view the problem in a relative sense and would not be adverse to securing marked improvements to the earnings position of their members relative to other groups of workers. On the other hand, the <u>raison d'être</u> of other unions, especially those representing skilled manual workers or white-collar staff, is to protect or even widen customary earnings differentials. The attempt to balance these conflicting objectives in a unified policy on low pay perhaps explains the apparently contradictory call, which the TUC has made on more than one occasion, both for relative improvements to the earnings position of the lowest paid, and for the preservation of established differentials. Wootton argues that such a goal is not only difficult to achieve - 'indeed, to raise the lowest paid without upsetting differentials is a mathematical impossibility'. (6)

The TUC seems more willing to perceive the problem in relative terms where some narrowing of earnings between those at the top and bottom of the incomes hierarchy is envisaged as a solution. Hence in 1967, in the context of a discussion on incomes policy, it was stated that:

'The people who should be pushed forward fastest of all are those who by common consent are in the ranks of the low paid. Those who should be held back are mainly to be found in the ranks of the top ten per cent of the population who receive at least twenty-five per cent (and almost certainly a good deal more) of the nation's income including all non-wage incomes. These people have not been notably affected by incomes policy as it has operated so far'. (7)

Or again in 1972:

'It must be accepted that an improvement in the relative position of the lower paid means a narrowing down of the spread of earnings - not only between low paid workers and other workers, but between lower paid workers and everyone else. There is a need for a policy of redistribution to embrace all levels of incomes'. (8)

However, such pronouncements are normally confined to the realms of rhetoric and are seldom, if ever, presented as serious collective bargaining objectives. Indeed, Hyman and Brough argue that in respect to the choice of pay comparisons, the normal dimensions of trade union wage policy tend to endorse and reinforce, rather than challenge the overall structure of inequality. (9) Certainly the policies pursued against low pay have been unambitious in this respect and would seem to be aimed at achieving some reduction in the spread of pay at the lower end of the earnings distribution, with the primary objective of securing for low paid workers and their families a standard of living at least equivalent to the 'State poverty-line'.

2. RECENT POLICY AND STRATEGY

Recent trade union initiatives in relation to low pay may be conveniently categorised and discussed under six broad heads: incomes policy; fiscal and social policy; minimum wage legislation; collective bargaining policy; strategy in wages council sectors; and recruitment. As previous analysis has suggested little evidence of a significant improvement in the low pay problem in recent years, the discussion which follows considers in particular possible reasons for the limited impact of the various policies pursued.

A. Incomes policy

It has been observed that the low paid actually lost ground during the period of policies administered by the NBPI, and there is little

to suggest that they fared better under later policies. The Labour
Government's policy of 1978, for example, permitted exceptional
increases for low paid workers where the resulting earnings were less
than £44.50 a week, a figure said to represent the TUC's low pay
target for 1974-75 of £30, updated by the maximum increases available
under subsequent policies. However, in April 1974, £30 represented
66.5% of average weekly male manual earnings whereas in April 1978,
£44.50 represented only 52.5%. (10) This implies that those workers
earning close to the TUC's minimum target in 1974 would have lost
ground by 1978 if their earnings had increased solely by the maximum
amounts available under later policies.

The failure of trade union initiatives in this area may, as
suggested in the previous chapter, reflect the priority accorded to
productivity over low pay as the main ground for exceptional increases
under successive policies. A second reason is that policies have not
always secured the full support of trade unions. Not all unions, it
has been observed, are in favour of measures designed to improve the
relative position of the lower paid. This is especially so when such
measures are proposed in the context of an incomes policy and where
priority for the low paid is implicitly or explicitly conditional upon
other groups of workers exercising a measure of wage restraint, or
accepting some narrowing of their pay differentials. In general,
unions which have been most disposed to some form of incomes policy
(at least under a Labour Government) are those representing large
groups of lower paid workers, particularly in the public sector,
whose members have tended to gain less from free collective bargaining
in the past. Those most opposed tend to operate in the private sector
and represent groups of skilled manual and professional employees.
This division is suggested in Table 6.1 which shows how the twenty
largest unions voted on whether to continue to observe the 12 month
interval between pay settlements in support of the Labour Government's
pay policy of July 1977-78. With the exception of the POEU all the
public sector services unions voted for the 12 month rule while the
unions voting against mainly included those representing professional
staff in (predominantly) private industry (ASTMS, APEX), and skilled
manual workers (NUM, SOGAT, ASBSBSW). The TGWU, while representing
large groups of lower paid workers, is a union which has always
tended to oppose policies of restraint.

It is unclear, however, to what extent successive policies would
have improved low pay even had they secured the full support of the
trade union movement. The apparent rationale underlying the low pay
provisions of recent policies, that restraint on the part of better
paid workers will benefit the lower paid, is not self-evident. Within
major bargaining groups this mechanism could operate, especially where
unions are organised on an industrial basis and are able to influence
the distribution of the wage bill among differing groups of workers
(e.g. coal mining). (11) However, no adequate machinery exists
generally which ensures that restraint on the part of higher paid
bargaining groups (e.g. printers) are transferred to lower paid
bargaining groups (e.g. wages council workers), rather than to the
profits of employers. Moreover, Cliff points out that the low paid
have tended to benefit most in relative terms during periods of
unfettered collective bargaining:

'If a worker in a strong position gets a small wage rise,
the one in the weaker position will get even less. This is
why wage differences within the working class have declined
considerably over the years as workers' strength grew:
skilled workers that were getting twice as much as the
unskilled for the years prior to 1914 were only 15 to 10
per cent ahead by the fifties in Britain ... It also explains
why wage differences are so large in the backward countries
where workers' organisation is poor and trade union rights
not secure'. (12)

TABLE 6.1   How the Twenty Largest Unions Voted on the 12 Month
Rule at the September 1977 TUC Congress

Trade Union	Membership (1,000)	How they voted on the 12 month rule
Transport Workers (TGWU)	1,930	against
Engineers (AUEW)	1,412	for *
Municipal Workers (GMWU)	916	for
Local Government (NALGO)	683	for
Public Employees (NUPE)	650	for
Electricians (EEPTU)	420	for
Shopworkers (USDAW)	413	for
Managerial staff (ASTMS)	396	against
Builders (UCATT)	294	for
Teachers (NUT)	289	for
Miners (NUM)	260	against
Civil Servants (CPSA)	231	for
Postmen (UPW)	201	for
Health workers (COHSE)	200	for
Printers (SOGAT)	194	against
Railwaymen (NUR)	180	for
Clerks (APEX)	142	for
Boilermakers (ASBSBSW)	128	against
Post Office Engineers (POEU)	126	against
Tailors (NUTGW)	113	against

*   Engineers: The 1.2 million strong engineering section of the AUEW
    voted for the 12 month rule, as did the small foundry section,
    but the white-collar and construction sections voted against.
Source: The Economist, 10th September 1977, p. 23.

A third limitation of incomes policy is that the low paid, especially
those in weakly organised or inefficient industries, rarely receive
the full amounts available under the policies. For example, only 7 out
of 50 wages councils succeeded in negotiating the maximum threshold
payments permitted under the Wilson Government's 1974 pay policy. (13)
    Finally, even were they to receive the maximum amounts available
under policies, this does not guarantee a relative or even absolute
improvement in the living standards of low earners and their families.
Increases in earnings may be offset through the effects of the poverty

trap. Under the Wilson Government's Stage I policy, for example, the
Low Pay Unit estimated that the flat-rate £6 limit could have meant a
reduction in living standards for a two-child family whose working
head was earning less than £40 a week in mid-1975. (14)

B. Fiscal and social policy

The TUC has mounted pressure for various changes in the area of fiscal
and social policy as part of its overall strategy towards low pay and
family poverty. Pressure has been applied through two main channels:
via general consultative procedures through which the TUC's views on
a range of economic and social issues have been made known to
governments (e.g. by means of its detailed pre-budget submissions to
Chancellors); and more directly, in the context of discussions on
incomes policies, where the TUC has made its co-operation conditional
upon certain modifications to social and fiscal arrangements (e.g.
Social Contract).

TUC policies have been of two sorts: those directed towards
improvements in the fields of indirect taxation and 'universal' social
benefits (e.g. pensions, family allowances); and policies relating to
direct taxation and means-tested benefits (e.g. FIS) which the TUC has
pursued in response to the poverty trap. This distinction is of
importance. Except in the broader context of incomes policy, policies
in the former area are generally unrelated to efforts directed through
the collective bargaining process to improve the living standards of
low earners and their families, since indirect taxes and universal
benefits do not vary as a worker's earnings increase. The development
of the poverty trap on the other hand has directly challenged the
ability of trade unions to raise the living standards of low earners
through normal collective bargaining activity.

Policies of the first sort have been fairly straightforward and
have met with some success. For example, the TUC has always maintained
as priority policy issues, the raising of family allowances and their
extension to the first child, increases in the level of retirement
pensions, and improvements to social and welfare benefits generally.
Campaigns have also been mounted in opposition to proposed cuts in
public expenditure, and the 'Social Wage'. In the field of indirect
taxation the TUC has, for example, argued against the introduction –
in principle, form and level – of value added tax, because it
represents a fiscal levy more regressive than direct taxes and the
purchasing tax arrangements which preceded it.

In relation to the poverty trap, trade union pressure for modifications to direct taxation and benefits policy was first seriously
applied following the introduction of FIS in 1971, a measure which
greatly exacerbated the influence of the trap. In its 1971 Economic
Review the TUC expressed its 'strongest reservations about FIS as a
solution to the problem of inadequate incomes among wage earners' in
that it would 'comprise a direct and explicit subsidy to low wages,
and may have the effect in lower-paid industries of actually slowing
down the progress of improvements in wage levels'. Instead the
General Council called for 'radical improvements in the redistributive
effects of the tax/social benefits system' including an end to means-
testing, a rise in the tax threshold and the introduction of a wealth

tax. (15) Similar proposals to alleviate the effects of the trap were contained in subsequent Reviews published throughout the 1970s. The 1977 Review, for example, discussed the possibility of a reduced rate band of direct taxation, a £100 increase in the tax threshold and a proposal to make national insurance contributions tax deductable. (16)

In reviewing union policy towards the poverty-trap, however, Pond et al note that the TUC seemed to prefer to tackle the problem through wage bargaining:

'The TUC has up to now appeared too unwilling to take the taxation and benefits issue really seriously and to argue as strongly, if not more strongly, for changes in benefit policy as it does for wage increases. The lesson of the years 1971 to 1976 is that verbal recognition of a problem and requests for policy changes are not enough'. (17)

The authors suggest that greater emphasis was placed upon the need for higher gross wages than on changes in fiscal and social policies, because the latter approach was alien to the traditional activity of trade unions, which was to negotiate adequate wage rates. Moreover, there seemed to be some confusion in the minds of prominent union officials over the different effects of universal benefits such as family allowances, and means-tested benefits such as FIS, on a family's net income. Proposals for changes in direct taxation and means-tested benefits, while put forward as measures designed to restore the ability of trade unions to raise the living standards of low earners, were interpreted by some as advocating that trade unions should renounce their responsibilities altogether for the low paid. Hence, it was in response to such proposals that Jack Jones expressed reservations about 'making virtual state pensioners of hundreds of thousands of ordinary, healthy, men and women' and of bringing about 'a situation where workers will depend upon the goodwill and kindness of the State for major elements of their standard of living'. Charles Donnet and David Lipsey (GMWU) were similarly hostile and responded by asking whether trade unions should be negotiating wage cuts in future to finance such measures. (18)

Emphasis on wage bargaining as a solution to the trap is suggested by a trend towards the inclusion of direct taxation and benefits policy within the scope of collective bargaining. This development is apparent in the way a number of recent wage claims have been presented, where the aim has clearly been to raise net disposable income. For example, evidence submitted to the Wilberforce Inquiry into the miners' dispute in 1972 included a chapter on the effects of the poverty trap in support of the miners' claim. (19) Less celebrated examples include the claims submitted on behalf of local authority manual workers and on behalf of local authority salaried staff in 1977, 1978 and 1979, all of which were supported by analyses of the effects of poverty trap factors on members' living standards throughout the preceding year. It is difficult, however, to establish how strong this trend has been as wage claims are seldom published.

Such efforts on the wages front appear, however, to have met with little success, as pay settlements for the low paid have fallen far short of the level required to spring them from the trap. Indeed, it has been estimated that in 1974 a married man with three children and earning £25 would have needed a gross pay rise of 88% just to restore his net real pay to its 1973 level. With four children, and earning £30, he would have needed an 80% increase in gross pay. (20) It is unrealistic to suppose that employers would or could concede claims of this magnitude, and to this extent the emphasis on collective bargaining as a solution to the trap would seem to be misdirected.

C.   Statutory national minimum wage

Trade union pressure for the introduction of a statutory national minimum wage (NMW) as a solution to low pay was most apparent in the late 1960s. The TGWU, for example, initiated a campaign for a legal minimum in 1967. (21) On the evidence of resolutions put to Congress between 1967 and 1970, other unions which appeared to support this approach included USDAW, the GMWU and NUPE. Union pressure on this front was such that the Government felt obliged to set up an inter-departmental working party of civil servants to consider the economic and social implications of the proposal. Their report was published as a Green Paper in 1969. (22)

After 1970, however, trade union support for this measure appeared to decline. This reflected a souring of relationships between unions and governments following a number of government initiatives in the area of industrial relations law. In particular, the Labour Government's White Paper 'In Place of Strife' published in 1969, (23) and the Conservative Government's 1971 Industrial Relations Act were inter-preted by the union movement as an attack on free collective bargaining, and thereafter unions began to equate any statutory involvement in industrial relations as an attack on their freedom.

Suspicion over statutory involvement was apparent in the section of the TUC's 1970 discussion document which dealt with the NMW proposal:

'However, a further and more important argument against a statutory minimum is that the trade union movement would in effect be inviting the State to intervene on a much bigger scale in the wage fixing process without having prior assurance that a statutory minimum would in fact be introduced and thereafter maintained at a level anywhere near what would be considered acceptable. The fact that Governments have not given Wages Councils more positive objectives in their terms of reference lends support to the view that the State would take a restrictive view of its role in taking the lead in tackling the problem of low pay. On the contrary, Governments have shown a propensity to impose negative restraints on Wages Councils, notably in the context of incomes policy'. (24)

These fears seemed to be shared by a majority of affiliated unions which commented upon the discussion document. No union was opposed in principle to some form of national minimum but 'most were opposed to a minimum wage taking a statutory form, at least until alternative methods had been tried'. (25) Most unions favoured a voluntary minimum along the lines of a TUC declaration or target and this was adopted as policy. There was little revival of support for the proposal after 1970, and at the 1974 Congress a call by Alan Fisher for a legal minimum, made on the ground that 'alternative methods' had indeed been tried and failed, was defeated by a large majority. (26)

This brief sketch raises two related questions: were union fears over the role of the State in the operation of an NMW valid grounds for failing to support the proposal?; and how effective could an NMW have been as a means of overcoming low pay had it been introduced in Britain?

In respect to the former question, proponents of the approach have argued that the union movement's misgivings rested on a political misunderstanding of the role which law could play in achieving trade union objectives. For example, in illustrating the dangers of over-relying on 'voluntary methods', Fisher and Dix drew parallels between the TUC's approach to low pay and the way it had handled the equal pay issue. At no point during the long period in which the TUC had advocated equal pay was there a decision to switch tactics from voluntary to legislative action. Then, when virtually confronted with a legislative initiative by Barbara Castle in 1969, it actually criticised the provision of the Equal Pay Bill for not going far enough or fast enough '- without apparently realizing that such a position was an admission that its previous policies had failed'. (27) Furthermore, it was argued that there was no obvious reason why a legal minimum should, in any case, be the sole responsibility of the State. Rather, a system could be devised whereby a minimum could be established and maintained within the collective bargaining process through annual tripartite negotiations between a strengthened TUC and representatives of the government and CBI, an approach with the 'outstanding merit' of ensuring direct and ongoing union involvement in the maintenance of an acceptable minimum.

Cliff, on the other hand, argues that fear over state involvement in industrial relations was not the 'real reason' for trade union opposition to the NMW solution:

'John Boyd's excuse (AUEW leader) used at the 1973 Labour Party Conference, that trade unions oppose on principle government interference with collective bargaining, won't wash - one can oppose anti-working class laws and still demand the eight-hour day. The real reason the TUC does not press for a statutory minimum wage is because to do so would be to put a Labour government on the spot. And it is for this reason that the 'Social Contract' does not call for a statutory minimum wage, and contains only a vague statement of intent'. (28)

Were it to be employed, the effectiveness of a NMW would largely depend on the level at which it was set. If set at a level determined by criteria similar to those employed in the present study in formulating a definition of low pay, perhaps its most beneficial effect would be to reduce drastically low pay among women, a majority of whom earned below £45 in April 1976 (Figure 2.1). Hence, an NMW could considerably bolster equal pay legislation which seems to have been rather ineffective in raising the pay of women relative to that of men (Table 2.5). A further advantage, even if set at a level considerably below, say, the lowest decile of male weekly or hourly earnings, is that it could eliminate the most extreme cases of under-payment and exploitation in certain sectors of employment where trade unionism is largely non-existent and unlikely to develop (e.g. private domestic service, among homeworkers, certain parts of the catering trade). This is of course assuming adequate enforcement arrangements.

Against this must be weighed the possible economic repercussions of the introduction of a NMW. The analysis in previous chapters provides some clues as to the limitations of the approach and the difficulties likely to be encountered. A few of the more obvious are listed below:

(i)   since low earners are concentrated in the small firm sector and in low productivity industries, the introduction of an NMW could create unemployment. Unemployment effects are likely to be particularly serious among women whose employment opportunities seem to be more adversely affected by conditions of inadequate labour demand than those of men (Table 4.1). Moreover, given that the low paid comprise high proportions of old and young employees, the unskilled and those in ill health, the proposal could tilt the labour market even further against these groups and reduce employment opportunities most for those least able to cope;

(ii)   unless offset by productivity increases, a NMW could increase unit costs and thus be inflationary. Items likely to increase fastest in price are those produced in low paying industries. Since these include industries and services dealing with the production and distribution of food (agriculture, fishing and retailing), and dealing in goods with low price or income elasticities of demand (textiles, clothing, retailing), price rises could be highest for those products with few substitutes and which figure most prominently in the budgets of low income groups;

(iii)   a NMW would be very inflationary if set at a level sufficient to eradicate low pay among men - say, at the lowest decile of male earnings. However, even this level would not offset fully the effects of the poverty trap (Figure 2.2). Hence, a NMW might do little to reduce family poverty;

(iv)   the introduction of a NMW would alter existing differentials and payment structures, and would therefore be opposed by certain trade unions. If such repercussions were to be avoided by, say, raising the earnings of all workers by a proportionate amount, the result would again be inflationary, and the relative earnings position of the low paid would not be improved.

Studies (mainly American) of the operation of minimum wage legis-lation in other countries lends support to a number of these objections, where increases in both unemployment (29) and prices (30) have been directly attributed to the introduction or raising of a legal minimum. Moreover, in reviewing international evidence, the NBPI found little to suggest that a NMW could secure any long-term improvement in the relative position of the low paid, as original differentials tended to reassert themselves within a year or so. (31)

Fisher and Dix argue, however, that such criticisms are only valid within the limited perspective in which they are perceived, and largely divorce the low pay problems from its political context. A NMW could be effective if accompanied by a number of radical measures to offset its effects on prices and employment, including government loans to industry, development grants, training and retraining programmes. These measures could be financed, it is argued, through a substantial redistribution of income and wealth achieved through union pressure on a 'revitalised' Labour Government geared to socialist policies. (32)

As was pointed out in Section 1, however, the objectives of trade union low pay policy do not generally extend to a political and economic challenge of this sort, and in sharp contrast to Fisher and Dix, the TUC argued in the 1970 discussion document that the accommodation of the economic consequences of a NMW would require curtailment of other trade union objectives:

> 'The introduction of a national minimum in effect would mean
> that the realisation of some other trade union objectives –
> whether straightforward pay increases, or improvements in
> conditions and fringe benefits, or more general objectives in
> the field of social services – would have to receive a
> relatively lower priority, and the higher the minimum the
> more certain this would be'. (33)

There seems to have been little support for the introduction of a NMW on this basis, which again would be inconsistent with the objectives of many powerful trade unions. If social services were to be affected, an approach of this sort might in any case do little to improve the general well-being of the low paid.

D. Collective bargaining policy

The TUC has periodically issued advice on how negotiators themselves might seek to assist the low paid when bargaining with employers. This has not taken the form of a list of general, standardised, collective bargaining priorities directed to solving low pay (e.g. the advocation of flat-rate increases). Instead, a pragmatic approach has been adopted whereby differing bargaining strategies have been put forward to meet differing sets of circumstances, with policy varying according to the influence of negotiators in differing bargaining settings and the pattern of low pay in the sectors for which they have responsibility.

Under the heading 'Collective Bargaining', the TUC, in its 1970 discussion document, distinguished two main types of bargaining situation: where agreements directly regulated the terms and conditions of all the workers covered (e.g. local firm agreements, national public sector agreements); and where actual conditions are mainly determined at a lower level (certain NJCs, JNCs, wages councils). Bargaining priorities in each case would differ, with negotiators in the direct bargaining situation having the greater range of options for tackling low pay.

In the former case, it was recommended that negotiators should initially examine in detail the specific causes of low pay for the workers concerned. The problem should then be tackled on two main fronts. First, great importance was placed upon seeking ways to increase the productivity and efficiency of the bargaining unit through, for example, the introduction of bonus incentive schemes or productivity bargaining, or by securing agreements governing the re-training of workers, the redefining of jobs and improvements to job content. Second, ways in which payments structures might be modified to assist the low paid should be considered, including for example, the substitution of higher basic rates for unreasonably high levels of overtime from which many low paid workers are unable to benefit (e.g. women, older workers, the handicapped), or by reviewing grading structures.

Negotiators in a 'dual' (e.g. national/local) bargaining setting on the other hand would have to ensure that agreements reached did not inhibit improvements which could be made at the lower bargaining level. In this respect the importance of negotiating minima rather than maxima was stressed. Policy should be directed towards securing marked improvements to basic rates, with relatively larger increases on bottom rates where a concertina effect on differentials could be avoided. Particular emphasis was placed upon negotiating minimum earnings guarantees as a method of concentrating pay increases on the lowest paid while reducing their repercussive impact on differentials.

In applying such policies, however, negotiators have also been advised to take account of the pattern of low pay appropriate to their sector. A common distinction in policy documents is between those sectors where pay levels are generally low, and those where average earnings are high but which contain significant pockets of low paid workers. (A similar distinction was drawn in Chapter 2). In the former case, the bargaining strategies deemed most appropriate have been of a general sort aimed at raising the average level of earnings in the sector as a whole, or improving the relative position of broad occupational groups representing a high proportion of the industry's total workforce. Recommended policies falling within this category have included: the negotiation of minimum earnings guarantees (especially in low paying sectors where seasonality and other forms of unpredictability of earnings exist, e.g. textiles); the intro-duction of PBR schemes and productivity agreements; the differentially favourable treatment of women within the terms of a settlement; and the negotiation of flat-rate 'across-the-board' increases.

In sectors where the low pay problem is relatively small, on the other hand, negotiators have been asked to apply policies of the more specific sort mentioned above, geared to reducing unfavourable labour market characteristics of particular groups of low paid workers or to redressing features of the payments structure which inhibit their earnings potential. Examples include: improving job content through regrading, training and extending promotion opportunities; eliminating lower rates or shortening unduly long salary scales which do not reflect differences in performance; reducing the age at which workers receive adult rates of pay or at least securing the application of the full negotiated increase to juvenile as well as adult rates; and the extension of incentive schemes to lower paid grades.

The above distinction reflects the TUC's attempt to resolve the 'mathematical impossibility' of improving the relative position of the lower paid while maintaining skill differentials. The stated aim of policies of the first sort has been to reduce inter-industry 'relativities', that is, earnings differences between low paid and more prosperous sectors, particularly between those of similar skill composition, an objective which unions have generally supported. In sectors where the low pay problem is relatively minor, however, such policies would have an unacceptable impact on differentials, and the TUC's explicit justification for applying policies of the second sort to these sectors has been to avoid or substantially reduce compression of skill differentials. (34)

A further distinction is often made between sectors where there is a wide dispersion of earnings and those where the spread in pay is relatively narrow. In the former, it is sometimes suggested that negotiators might wish to seek some tapering of pay increases percentage-wise so that those on the lowest grades can gain more proportionately, if not monetarily. This proposal is usually advanced with caution, however, and not thought appropriate for sectors where differentials are already very narrow and could not be compressed without creating anomilies (e.g. agriculture).

It is difficult to assess how far these recommendations have been followed or their potential for improving low pay. As regards productivity and efficiency considerations, it has been noted that the introduction of PBR schemes in the public sector appears to have alleviated the problem to some extent. However, it has also been shown that low productivity and low earnings coincide with the widespread use of incentive schemes in a number of low paying manufacturing industries, especially in clothing and footwear and in timber (Table 3.5 cf Table 3.13), so that for these sectors at least, the solution would not appear to lie in this direction. Indeed, the proponents of this approach perhaps overlook the relatively small contribution which output-related benefits make to average gross earnings in industry generally. As was shown in Table 3.13, PBR payments accounted for just 8% of average male manual earnings in 1976. Fisher and Dix argue that to extend such schemes to make any appreciable difference to the earnings of the low paid 'would demand a vigour not yet displayed by negotiators, and moreover, would undoubtedly require the kind of modifications in wage structures and bargaining arrangements which advocates of such methods seek to avoid'. (35)

Previous discussion has suggested further limitations to policies geared to improving productivity and efficiency. It has been noted throughout that low paying industries, especially service industries, are less susceptible to machinery-induced improvements to labour productivity. In addition, it was argued in Chapter 4 that increases in productivity may have an adverse effect on pay levels, by, for example, further reducing labour demand in low paying manufacturing industries or by contributing to a surplus of labour in the service sector. It has also been observed that the focus on increases productivity in recent incomes policies may have exacerbated the earnings position of the lower paid.

Of the other policies recommended, Moore, writing in 1976, cites as

examples of unions which have been especially active in pursuing
policies of the 'general' sort in low paying sectors (e.g. flat-rate
increases, minimum earnings guarantees), the TGWU, NUPE, APEX, USDAW
and SOGAT. He also notes that some unions which had hitherto been
very conscious of skill differentials, such as the Iron and Steel
Trades Confederation, had recently moved to flat-rate increases.
Unions cited as most active in pursuing policies of the more specific
sort to alleviate pockets of low pay (e.g. improved job content,
narrowing incremental scales) included UCATT, CPSA, ASTMS, the GMWU
and again the TGWU and NUPE. (36)

The application of tapering formulae seems to have been fairly widespread in the late 1960s. For example, the TUC reported their widespread application in settlements reached in 1969. (37) Thereafter,
however, the popularity of this bargaining approach appears to have
diminished. Indeed, Fels notes that recommendations for the
application of tapering formulae and pro tanto increases, while
initially an important element in the NBPI's low pay policy, were
later abandoned owing to trade union pressure. Opposition related to
the effects of such settlements on differentials. (38)

What is most apparent from this brief review is the extent to which
policy has focused on methods of improving low pay which have least
impact on differentials, a preoccupation which has possibly inhibited
the effectiveness of the policies pursued. This again reflects the
TUC's attempt to achieve a unified policy on low pay where union
objectives differ.

E.   Strategy in wages council sectors

The abolition of wages councils and their replacement by voluntary
collective bargaining has been an aim central to the TUC's low pay
policy. Reasons for trade union opposition to the wages council
system are many, those most commonly voiced being that: it has failed
to set adequate minimum rates in low paying sectors; minimum rates
are not adequately enforced; the system inhibits the development of
voluntary collective bargaining; statutory interference in wage
fixing is undesirable; wages councils have restricted terms of
reference and little influence on actual pay and conditions (as
opposed to minimum standards); and the system is open to abuse by
governments especially in the context of incomes policy.

While total abolition is the long-term aim, the TUC has also
considered policies for improving the scope, operation and effectiveness of wages councils, both as a means of hastening the achievement
of the long-term goal, and to improve employment conditions in these
sectors in the interim. The 1970 discussion document provides a good
example of this policy position, where it was argued that the wholesale or immediate abolition of councils could remove the only form
of protection for vulnerable groups of workers. Accordingly:

'... Wages Councils should be considered not so much as outmoded
pieces of machinery to be abolished as and when effective
alternatives are established – if this ever happens – but more
as pieces of (albeit inadequate) negotiating machinery that
need to be reformed and developed in stages towards the

achievement of the desired voluntary machinery'. (para. 46)

This 'reformative' element in the TUC's wages council policy was most apparent in the late 1960s - early 1970s, and included among those 'interim' reforms proposed or discussed were the following sorts of measures: reducing the number of wages councils and rationalising their field (including agreement by unions on 'spheres of influence' and the withdrawal by unions from industries where their interest is marginal); abolishing the anonymity of wages council representation so that unions became signatories to Orders: abolishing the system whereby the Minister appoints 'worker sides' and substituting selection by unions; the establishment of a joint secretariat from both sides of industry (as in voluntary machinery) to replace government appointees; an end to independent membership of wages councils; enhancing the role of wages councils to enable them to fix other terms and conditions besides wages and holidays; financial aid to unions organising in wages council sectors through a government financed 'Trade Union Development Scheme' (as proposed in 'In Place of Strife'); the establishment of joint trade union recruitment committees in groups of wages council industries to co-ordinate organising activities; and the amendment of Section 8 of the Terms and Conditions of Employment Act 1959 to permit a claim that 'recognised terms and conditions are not being observed' to be made by workers in wages council industries. (39) A number of these reforms were realised with the passing of the Employment Protection Act 1975. (40)

Unions were not, however, unanimous in their support for such measures and at the Post-Donovan Conference on the wages councils sector in 1969 a number of unions rejected all proposals of this sort in favour of a 'total abolitionist' position, arguing that reform to the system could prolong the existence of wages councils and were thus undesirable. A SOGAT delegate, for example, summarised his union's attitude as 'Don't mend it, end it', and a similar standpoint was adopted by delegates from the TGWU, the Bakers' union and the United Road Transport Union. On the other hand, delegates from the clothing and textile unions (NUTGW, UJFKTO), USDAW and the agricultural workers' union (NUAAW) saw a continuing role for wages councils and were sympathetic towards a number of the reforms proposed. These two camps seemed to be fairly evenly divided. (41) With respect to similar proposals contained in the 1970 discussion document the TUC also reported disagreement among unions over the future of councils, though the majority view seemed to favour an approach geared to the development and reform of the system towards a more positive bargaining function. (42)

The advent of the Conservative Government's Industrial Relations Act, however, appeared to influence union wages council policy in a manner and direction similar to its influence on the statutory minimum wage proposal, and after 1971 a relaxation of the reformative aspects of TUC policy was noticed, particularly those statutory elements, in favour of a stronger abolitionist position. (43) A strong emphasis in policy statements issued thereafter was that legislative reforms should not be imposed on trade unions and were only appropriate where they facilitated abolition:

'Any process which enhances or extends the <u>function</u> of a
wages council should be examined critically ... Amending
legislation may be needed to <u>facilitate abolition</u> where
this is considered necessary by, e.g. abolishing the need
to secure the employers' agreement to this step. Other
amendments might <u>permit</u> unions and management to appoint
their own representatives, <u>allow</u> council members to appoint
their own chairman and establish a joint secretariat drawn
from both sides of industry with the same powers as the
chairman and secretariat of a voluntary negotiating body ...
Existing legislative limits on the terms of reference of wages
councils should be relaxed to <u>enable</u> them, where necessary to
develop new functions - e.g. in relation to sick pay, or
pensions schemes or security developments. The <u>enabling</u> nature
of this legislation is important: in all cases the agreement
of the union side would be necessary before any of these
developments was actually allowed to take place'. (Their
emphasis) (44)

An important consequence of this shift in policy was that it
appeared to influence the recommendation of the Commission on
Industrial Relations (CIR), a body charged with the task, under the
1971 Act, of reviewing the workings of wages councils and recommending
abolition where appropriate. While trade unions withdrew their members
from the CIR in protest against the Act, the policy emphasis of the
CIR nevertheless 'reflected the trade unions' own growing opposition
to the existence of statutory machinery for establishing minimum rates
of pay'. (45) SOGAT, for example, boycotted proceedings leading to
the abolition of the Paper-Box Wages Council but, upon abolition,
published a pamphlet welcoming the decision. (46)

The terms of reference of the CIR allowed it to recommend whether a
council should be abolished or its scope of operation altered. The
main criterion used in deciding if abolition was appropriate was
whether the existence of the council was necessary to maintain a
reasonable standard of pay for workers within its scope. In
particular, the Commission examined the relationship between statutory
minimum rates (SMR) and actual rates of pay, and abolition was mostly
recommended where a majority of workers were being paid at least 10%
above the SMR and where 'satisfactory' collective bargaining
arrangements existed. Between 1971 and 1974 thirty out of the then
existing fifty-three councils were so examined. Abolition was
recommended in ten cases and amalgamation in a further fourteen.

The Low Pay Unit has been particularly critical of these decisions,
arguing that the Commission's recommendations did not pay due regard
to the size and interests of the 'vulnerable minority', that is,
those workers whose earnings were very close to the SMR and who were
not covered by collective bargaining. Table 6.2 below shows the size
of this vulnerable minority in councils recommended for abolition.

TABLE 6.2   'Vulnerable Minority' in Wages Councils Recommended
             for Abolition by the CIR

Wages council	Vulnerable minority as % of all workers (1)	% of firms with collective bargaining
Industrial and Staff Canteens	5 (2)	45
Hollow-ware	10	60
Keg and Drum	1.5	33
Pin, Hook and Eye (3)	8	80
Stamped or Pressed Metals	12	33
Boot and Floor Polish	3 (2)	22
Ready Made Tailoring	6	46
Shirtmaking	10	43
Rubber-Proofed Garment	15	30
Corset	23	39
Paper Box	12	55
Total size of vulnerable minority	30,500 workers	

(1) Vulnerable minority = % of employees within the scope of the
    wages council whose actual rates of pay were less than 10%
    above the statutory minimum rate.
(2) Estimated figures.
(3) Abolition for factory workers only - strictly a change in
    scope - not abolition.
Source: Low Pay Bulletin No.2, Low Pay Unit, March 1975, Table 1,
        p. 2. (Data originally gathered from CIR Reports Nos. 27,
        47-51, 77, 83, HMSO, 1972-74).

Winyard argues that these figures demonstrate that the CIR, and
trade unions in their tacit support of the CIR approach, seriously
misjudged the sorts of policies required for dealing with low pay in
wages council sectors. For example, in only two of the ten councils
recommended for abolition were more than 50% of firms within the scope
of collective bargaining. It was also pointed out that wages council
sectors are precisely those where it is most difficult to extend
collective bargaining owing to the traditional recruitment problems
associated with female-dominated, turnover-prone, small firm sectors.
Moreover, the figure for the vulnerable minority of 30,500 workers
was not considered a true reflection of the seriousness of low pay in
these sectors, as SMRs are set at 'pathetically low' levels. In the
Industrial and Staff Canteen sector, for example, the lowest minimum
rate was £12.46 in 1974 - less than half the TUC's minimum weekly wage
target. For these reasons, he suggests that the decision to recommend
abolition of the ten councils (six of which were subsequently
abolished) was premature, and that a more appropriate approach would
have been to extend the scope and improve the effectiveness of wages

councils in the short-term and to set a minimum target level of
coverage for collective bargaining to be reached before abolition.
In consequence of the approach adopted, however, 'trade unions will
have to mount massive recruitment campaigns if the low paid are not
to suffer'. (47) The achievements of trade unions in this respect are
briefly considered below.

F.   Recruitment

As noted above, trade unions have recently placed policy emphasis on
recruitment and the extension of collective bargaining coverage as
the major means of tackling low pay in the wages council sector.
Greater effort on the recruitment front has always, however, been an
important element in the TUC's low pay policy, given the low levels
of union density in low paying industries.

As regards the wages council sector, there does not appear to be
any recent statistical data from which to evaluate how successful
trade unions have been in expanding membership. In 1976, however, a
survey conducted by the Low Pay Unit among unions organising in those
councils recommended for abolition revealed 'a lack of any major new
initiatives on the recruitment front' in terms of additional resources
devoted to recruitment or the establishment of monitoring systems to
check recruitment progress among low paid workers. (48)

Perhaps the most comprehensive account of collective bargaining
developments following the abolition of a council is contained in a
recent study of the Paper Box industry commissioned by the Department
of Employment, which was based on a survey of pay and conditions in
the industry undertaken in 1977-78. (49) The CIR recommended the
abolition of the Paper Box Wages Council not on the usual ground that
wages were in practice much higher than the legal minimum rates, but
in the belief that the British Paper Box Association (BPBA) used the
existence of the council as an excuse for not entering into direct
collective bargaining. However, the final decision to abolish the
council was only taken after assurances from the trade unions involved
to devote additional resources to recruitment in unorganised sectors.
The above study fulfilled a further stipulation that there should be
a follow-up survey two years after abolition to investigate
developments.

The survey found evidence of attempts by unions to organise workers
after abolition, but reported that these were largely unsuccessful,
particularly in the smallest and least organised firms, and out of
twenty-one recorded attempts to increase union membership only seven
resulted in any long-term increase. This was partly the fault of the
trade unions involved (SOGAT and the GMWU) who failed to reach an
appropriate 'spheres of influence' agreement to avoid wasteful
duplication of recruitment efforts in the same geographical areas.
Moreover, unions wrongly believed that the small unorganised firms
had all but disappeared since abolition and with them the need for a
sustained recruitment drive.

However, the major blame for the limited success of the post-
abolition recruitment drives was attributed to the employers. Union
efforts were hampered by the refusal of the BPBA to release the names
of its members, even although it had concluded a voluntary collective

bargaining agreement with SOGAT and the GMWU upon abolition in 1975. Efforts were further frustrated by the 'exceedingly hostile' attitude to trade unions found amongst individual employers, some of whom threatened to close the factory if the union came in, cut privileges (e.g. time off to go to the dentist) or reduce wages to a fictional 'union rate'. One employer distributed £5 notes to workers immediately before a trade union recruitment approach. The report noted that these tactics were generally encouraged by the BPBA, indicating a lack of genuine commitment to voluntary collective bargaining.

As regards the impact of abolition on pay levels, the survey generally confirmed the worst fears of the Low Pay Unit. In at least three firms not covered by collective bargaining, payments were found to be lower than would have been likely under wages council control. Furthermore, a high proportion of firms theoretically covered by the BPBA's agreement failed to implement its minimum terms, or unilaterally modified the terms of the agreement to suit their own circumstances and to the detriment of the lower paid. This situation was directly attributed to the failure of trade unions to penetrate unorganised sectors, and to the fact that neither the Association nor the unions had established a 'policing' system. Accordingly, underpayment was found to be just as common in all those sectors of the industry identified as being low paid by the CIR, and the report concluded that 'there is little evidence that the abolition of the Paper Box Wages Council provided any benefits which could justify the removal of protection against low pay - protection still required by a minority of the labour force'. (50)

It is unclear how typical has been the experience of the Paper Box industry.* Bosanquet notes, however, that some progress has been made in extending collective bargaining in catering, one of the lowest paid and least organised wages council industries. For example, collective bargaining has become well established since nationalisation in British Transport Hotels. In the private sector, the GMWU has recently reached agreements with Berni Inns, Grand Metropolitan, Crest-Esso and Scottish and Newcastle Breweries. Moreover, he notes that the TGWU and GMWU have recently signed 'spheres of influence' agreements governing catering workers to enhance recruitment efforts. (51)

Certainly, if viewed in the long term, the impact of union recruitment activity in wages council industries has been unimpressive. Price and Bain's analysis showed that for most low paying industries in which wages councils are prominent, union density in 1974 (as outlined in Table 3.12) differed little from that in 1948. In agriculture, timber and distribution, union density actually declined

---

* Since writing, the Department of Employment has published the second of its studies in this series, relating to the Cutlery Wages Council. The main findings and conclusions were largely identical to those in respect of the Paper Box Wages Council, and the study recommended the re-establishment of some form of social control of wages and conditions in the industry. See C. Craig <u>et al</u>, Abolition and after : the Cutlery Wages Council, <u>Research Paper No.18</u>, Department of Employment, January 1981.

over the post-war period, though some increases in density occurred in clothing, footwear and leather. (52)

Greater progress appears to have been made, however, in those low paying industries outside the wages council sector, especially among white-collar employees in low paying service sectors and among both manual and non-manual employees in the public sector. The growth in white-collar unionism is most noticeable from the mid-1960s. Price and Bain's figures showed that the percentage of white-collar employees who were unionised increased from some 30% in 1964 to nearly 40% in 1974. This indicates vigorous recruitment activity on the part of white-collar unions, bearing in mind the expansion of employment in white-collar sectors of employment since the mid-1960s. This is borne out by TUC union membership statistics which show, for example, that the National Union of Bank Employees increased its membership by 82% between 1964 and 1975. Over the same period the increase in NALGO membership was 85%. Between 1968 and 1975 membership of ASTMS more than tripled. Large increases in membership also occurred in the (predominantly) manual public sector unions, NUPE and COHSE, which recorded increases of 144% and 161% respectively between 1964 and 1975. (53)

These figures demonstrate considerable achievement on the part of unions in some low paying industries in responding to changes in the distribution and composition of employment. Such efforts are of particular relevance to the low pay problem if credence is accorded to the analyses of Rubery and Braverman discussed in Chapter 4, and require to be maintained and extended if the sorts of processes described by these authors are to be arrested.

3. SUMMARY AND CONCLUSIONS

The trade union movement has recently devoted serious efforts towards tackling low pay in Great Britain. The problem has been attacked on a number of different fronts, demonstrating some awareness of its complexities and a willingness to respond to new developments as they arise. Not all unions, however, have favoured measures designed to solve low pay, and the support of individual unions for policies proposed to pursued has varied according to the types of workers represented, industries covered and political viewpoints held by union leaders. The TUC's attempt to achieve a unified low pay policy acceptable to unions with differing and possibly opposing objectives has influenced the way in which the problem has been defined and tackled. Accordingly, the objectives of policy have been somewhat modest with the main problem defined as one of poverty rather than inequality, a distinction difficult to sustain and implying little commitment (at least at the level of the TUC) to a reduction in the overall pattern of inequality as part of a broader political strategy against low pay. The priority accorded to the maintenance of skill differentials has strongly influenced the general direction of policies and compromised the effectiveness of policy initiatives in a number of the areas discussed. Serious shortcomings have been high-lighted, however, in virtually all the policies pursued, and it has been suggested that trade union action in some areas (e.g. incomes policy, productivity, wages council policy) may have exacerbated the problem. In other areas, policies followed suggest the failure of union leaders to grasp (or acknowledge) the political significance of the low pay problem (e.g. in respect to the statutory minimum wage proposal) or to comprehend fully its complexities (e.g. in the area of fiscal/social policy). Taken together, the policies and strategies pursued appear as yet to have made little impact on the problem.

CONCLUDING COMMENTS

The low pay problem does not easily lend itself to analytical scrutiny. Its potential scope is as wide as that of wage determination in general, and it is not possible to deal adequately with the topic in isolation from a consideration of its broader economic, political and social context. In pursuing its objectives, this study has sought to distinguish fact from fiction, clarify the main issues involved and provide further insight into the major dimensions of the problem.

Perhaps one of the most important general points which the early part of the discussion highlights is the need to define and measure the problem and its characteristics with some degree of care and precision. The scope and complexity of the topic demands a rigorous approach, and there appears to have been some tendency in past work to derive overgeneral conclusions from a restricted data base. In wading through the evidence, some care has been taken to avoid the major statistical pitfalls, and the study has produced a number of results which challenge widely accepted views and qualify previous findings. For example, low pay does not appear to be a major direct source of poverty except in families containing children, though its indirect contribution to poverty is perhaps greater than often supposed. Nor is the pattern of low pay simply or generally related to skill patterns. Industries where employment is contracting are not generally or even mostly those which pay the lowest wages. Neither does evidence indicate that low paying industries are generally inefficient in their use of resources. Only in employing particular (and not necessarily the most appropriate) definitions of efficiency can this be shown to be generally the case.

In the past, a tendency to generalise and oversimplify the issue was difficult to avoid on account of data limitations. Until very recently, major emphasis appears to have been placed on the incidence of low pay in manufacturing industries and among full-time male manual employees, areas where data were most available. However, this study has shown the problem to be more prevalent in the service sector of the economy, among women and among part-time employees. Moreover, it has been shown that important differences exist between the manu-facturing and service sectors with regard to the causes of low pay. In these respects it is hoped that the study has complemented other efforts recently made towards redressing a hitherto unbalanced and partial approach to the problem.

Data limitations persist, however, as has been made apparent throughout the discussion. The service sector in particular continues to be neglected. For example, Census information on 'Distribution and Other Services' is much less comprehensive than that relating to the production sector of the economy. This disparity is not warranted on the grounds of the relative employment size of each sector and their respective contribution to economic activity, or, indeed, in the light of the recent employment trends and developments in economic structure which have been discussed. Data on womens' pay is a further area in need of improvement. Though women now constitute some 40% of total employment, the Department of Employment continues to publish less detailed NES information on the earnings of women than of men. Information on the earnings of part-time women is particularly scarce. Such omissions require to be rectified if this and related topics are to be accorded treatment at the level of detail they demand.

The interactive and dynamic features of the low pay problem have been strong themes throughout the discussion. With respect to the former, it has been shown that while many different factors contribute to low pay, they do not act independently. Approaches to the problem which assign greater explanatory importance to one set of variables over another break the logical continuum and can be misleading. As regards the latter, rather too much emphasis appears to have been placed in recent studies upon the stability of earnings patterns. Considerable stability does exist in the pattern of inter-personal, inter-industry and inter-occupational differentials. However, it has also been shown that the relative size or importance of the low pay problem in differing sectors of the economy, or among different categories of employees, is closely related to developments in economic structure, and may quickly alter in line with changes in the composition and distribution of employment.

Recognition of this dynamic element to the problem allows deeper insight into the causes of low pay. Wages may be determined by supply and demand but what determines supply and what determines demand are questions too often neglected in treatment given to the topic. The study has touched upon a number of the issues involved and further research requires to be undertaken in this area if the full economic, and indeed political, implications of the low pay problem are to be clarified.

On the trade union response, the study has gathered together evidence not previously assembled in systematic fashion, and attempted to show how the pattern of response has been influenced by a combination of economic, political and social developments in post-war Britain. The emergence of trade union concern over low pay in the mid-1960s did not seem to originate 'spontaneously' from with the trade union movement, but rather was prompted by developments in public policy, in particular, by the attempts of the Labour Government to achieve a viable form of incomes policy which would secure the general support of trade unions. The subsequent application of the policies formulated, together with developments in social and fiscal policy, changes in union leadership and the 'rediscovery' of poverty by academics and others, sustained and enhanced trade union interest in the topic and elevated the low pay problem to a distinct policy issue in its own right.

As yet, however, trade unions appear to have made little impact on the problem, and in highlighting some of the weaknesses of policies recently pursued, the discussion has attempted to provide some pointers as to how the effectiveness of the response might be improved. For example, policy in relation to the poverty-trap is likely to remain unsuccessful until trade unions place more emphasis upon securing appropriate modifications to direct taxation and social benefits policy. Or again, in respect to the wages council sector, a more effective approach might place greater emphasis upon reforming rather than abolishing the system. In these and other areas of response, for example, in respect to the statutory minimum proposal, the effectiveness of policies might also benefit from a review of political perspectives on the role which law can play in achieving trade union objectives.

Weakness of leadership at the centre of the trade union movement, however, perhaps represents the major impediment to an effective trade union response. The complexity of the low pay problem is such that it demands a co-ordinated approach on the part of the trade union movement as a whole, directed centrally by a leadership capable of implementing clear policy objectives. The hallmark of TUC low pay policy, on the other hand, has been one of compromise and accommodation, with the problem defined in a vague if not inconsistent fashion, and policy initiatives tempered in the interests of unity. Where conflicting objectives in respect to low pay remain unresolved, however, and no clear lead is taken at leadership level, a 'unified' approach of this sort can offer little challenge to the <u>status quo</u>.

This is best illustrated by the failure of the TUC to acknowledge and confront the central economic and political issues posed by low pay. A minimal objective of low pay policy, as implied by TUC policy statements, would seem to be that of raising the incomes of all low earners and their families to a level at least equal to that which can be attained by families relying on State benefits. However, to achieve even this relatively modest goal would require additional resources of considerable magnitude. This raises a simple but fundamental question - where is the money to come from? One possible source is the low paid themselves through increased productivity, though it has been observed that there are important limitations to what may be achieved in this direction. Profits represent an alternative source and there is certainly some scope for trade unions to gain further concessions in those more profitable low paid sectors, for example, in certain parts of the catering trade. However, as a majority of low paid workers are to be found in small-firm, low-productivity industries, and in the public sector, it must be accepted that there are basic economic constraints to solving low pay, both in respect to individual undertakings and from the point of view of the economy as a whole.

In this respect, a serious challenge to low pay would need to take one of two forms. On the one hand, trade unions can refuse to accept the legitimacy or inevitability of these economic obstacles by pursuing an overtly political campaign of the sort favoured by those more radical elements of the union movement, directed towards securing fundamental changes to the distribution of income and wealth and an alternative economic order capable of providing a socially acceptable minimum standard of living for all. Alternatively, a solution can be sought within the present confines of political economy, by accepting that improvements to low pay may only be gained at the expense of other current trade union priorities or objectives. If levels of employment and social services are to be maintained, this latter approach must necessarily involve a considerable measure of wage restraint on the part of better-paid workers, with concomitant savings transferred to the low paid through a combination of existing and new forms of machinery. Possible mechanisms include incomes policy, minimum wage legislation, fiscal measures (including subsidies to low paying sectors) and via collective agreements.

Whether the broad spectrum of interests and political perspectives represented within the trade union movement can ever be channelled towards a concerted attack on low pay along either of these lines raises a number of complex issues outwith the scope of this book. What does seem certain, however, is that the 'pragmatic' approach so far adopted by the official leadership, based on accommodation rather than resolution of divisions, will continue to achieve little.

POSTSCRIPT

THE 1980s - DEVELOPMENTS AND PROSPECTS

Observers of industrial relations and the labour market will be aware
how quickly the course of events may alter. This is especially so on
the wages front during periods of rapid inflation, when published
earnings data become unrepresentative within short periods. The
statistical analysis of earnings patterns contained in this study
relied for the most part on data relating to April 1976, and to this
extent must be viewed as an historical account. However, in the light
of past movements in earnings structures, as discussed in Chapter 2,
it would be surprising if the present pattern of low pay differed
significantly from that in 1976. This is confirmed in Table P.1 in
respect to low paying industries, the main statistical basis upon
which the analyses in Chapters 3 and 4 were developed and conclusions
on the causes of low pay derived. The figures are directly comparable
with those contained in Table 3.1, and show that the ten lowest
paying industries in April 1980 were as in April 1976, with only minor
changes to ranking.

Of recent economic and social developments pertaining to low pay,
perhaps the single most important has been the unprecedented increase
in unemployment. Between November 1975 and November 1980, registered
unemployment in Great Britain increased by 84%. This is an accelerating trend, and in the first eleven months of 1980 alone, unemployment increased by 47% to top the two million mark. (1) By
March 1981, this had increased to 2.5 million and present estimates
predict a startling 3 million unemployed by the end of the year.
Clearly, this worrying trend increases greatly the economic obstacles
to solving low pay, especially in the small firm sectors most prone
to bankruptcy, and may also possibly reduce the priority accorded to
the problem within the union movement, where the fight against unemployment is likely to overshadow other trade union objectives in
the foreseeable future.

Recent developments in public policy have been no more encouraging,
and the problem of low pay and poverty appears to be far down the
list of priorities of the present Thatcher Government, as indicated,
for example, by the fiscal adjustments it introduced upon assuming
office. Reducing standard and upper rates of direct taxation and

compensating through increases to indirect taxation is a formula of obvious disadvantage to low earners. Moreover, the present Government has gained the dubious honour of being the first in post-war history to cut the real value of unemployment benefits, thereby preventing the unemployed from escaping their 'fair share' of the sacrifices demanded by the recession. Furthermore, the pursuance of monetarist economic policies in preference to incomes policy as a means of curbing inflation, together with the low level of rapport and co-operation characterising TUC/Government relations, has rendered the current social climate less conducive to raising or debating the low pay issue, a situation which may lead to a reduction in public awareness of the problem.

TABLE P.1   Industries with the Lowest Level of Average Gross Weekly Earnings for Full-time Manual Men - April 1980

Industry	Average gross weekly earnings (£)
All industries and services	111.7
All manufacturing industries	115.2
Agriculture, forestry and fishing	87.8
Clothing and footwear	91.0
Miscellaneous services	92.8
Distributive trades	96.0
Textiles	98.4
Public administration and defence	99.7
Professional and scientific services	100.0
Timber and furniture	104.2
Insurance, banking and finance	106.6
Leather, leather goods and fur *	na

* Census data relating to 1978 again show that the level of average male manual earnings in this Order was below that of all other manufacturing Orders other than clothing and footwear. Business Monitor PA1000, Census of Production 1978, Provisional Results, Department of Industry, HMSO, 1980, Table 1.

Source: New Earnings Survey 1980, Department of Employment, December 1980, Part C, Table 54.

In view of these developments, particularly that of unemployment, the present period must surely represent a watershed in trade union policy on the low pay issue. It is difficult to envisage how trade unions can continue to pursue actively policies against low pay if, as suggested, unemployment becomes the primary issue of trade union concern. Indeed, it is possible that the continuance of the economic decline will be accompanied by the disappearance of the topic of low pay as a major trade union policy issue. It is also possible, of course, that events may produce the opposite effect and encourage trade unions to tackle the problem more actively along with unemployment in the context of some broader political challenge to government policy and the economic <u>status quo</u>.

NOTES AND REFERENCES

Chapter 2

1. Surveys were conducted in both Britain and Ireland. For a description of the findings, see H. Behrend and A. Knowles, What is lower pay?, SSRC Newsletter 8, SSRC, March 1970, pp. 19-21; H. Behrend et al, Views on Pay Increases, Fringe Benefits and Low Pay, Economic and Social Research Institute Paper No. 56, Dublin, August 1970; H. Behrend, What is lower pay? - 1971 follow-up survey, SSRC Newsletter 12, SSRC, June 1971, pp. 5-7; H. Behrend, Attitudes to Price Increases and Pay Claims, NEDO Monograph 4, NEDO, 1974, pp. 49-56.
2. H. Behrend (1974), op.cit., p. 54.
3. NBPI, Report No. 169, General Problems of Low Pay, Cmnd. 4648, HMSO, 1971, para. 9.
4. Royal Commission on the Distribution of Income and Wealth, Report No. 6, Lower Incomes, Cmnd. 7175, HMSO, 1978, para. 3.15. Hereinafter referred to as the 'Royal Commission'.
5. NBPI (1971), op.cit., para. 111.
6. ibid., para. 12.
7. The Low Pay Unit is an independent pressure group established with funds from the Seebohm Rowntree Studentship Fund. Its main function, as described in its initial publication, is 'to draw attention to the extent of low pay, and its concentration in the wages council sector'. Low Pay Bulletin No. 1, Low Pay Unit, January 1975, p. 1.
8. Low Pay Bulletin No. 1, op.cit., p. 1.
9. Department of Employment, New Earnings Survey 1976, HMSO, 1977.
10. Figures from NES (1976), op.cit., Part A, Table 15.
11. The figure is made up as follows: long-term scale rate for married couple in April 1976 (£21.55) + £4.75 for each child = £31.05. Child rates vary by child age. The £4.75 figure was obtained by adding together the rates payable for each age band below 18 years and dividing by the number of age bands.
12. These figures derive from DHSS estimates published in Hansard, 15th October 1976, p. 249, in response to a question tabled by Ralph Howell MP.
13. 'Full-time' employees are defined in the survey as those whose

normal weekly hours exceed 30. 'Adults' are defined as men aged 21 and over and women aged 18 and over. The definitions of 'manual' and 'non-manual' adopted in the NES are those of the CODOT occupational classification system. For details of the CODOT system, see NES (1976), op.cit., Part A, Appendix 2.

14. These and subsequent figures of estimated numbers of employees by occupational group (June 1976) from Royal Commission, op.cit., Table M.7, p. 259. Corresponding figures for April 1976 were unavailable.

15. High as these figures may seem, it has been argued that the incidence of low pay is more extensive than is apparent from NES data. Townsend, for example, points out that the low paid tend to be underrepresented in the NES sample owing to the exclusion of economically active, but intermittently unemployed, groups of workers (up to a fifth of wage earners) 'who are bound to include a disproportionate number of the lowest paid'. This, together with the return of information by employers rather than earners themselves, tends to inflate NES earnings figures. From NES 1968, he found that earnings at the lowest decile were up to 3.5% higher for full-time men and 14% higher for full-time women than those recorded in the Family Expenditure Survey and in his own 'poverty survey', which both covered roughly the same period. P. Townsend, Poverty in the UK, Penguin, 1979, pp. 621-23.

16. Had it been possible to employ the £1.05 definition the numbers and percentages of low paid part-time employees would have been considerably higher than shown. Approximately 0.45 million part-time women (13%) and 0.07 million part-time men (10%) had gross hourly earnings between the range £1.00 to £1.10 in April 1976.

17. Since the data in all columns are expressed as percentages, terminological difficulties can occur in distinguishing the two phenomena. To avoid these, the text which follows refers to the figures in Columns 1 and 3 as indicating the relative concentrations of low earners by industry, and the figures in Columns 2 and 4 as indicating the relative numbers of low earners by industry.

18. This and subsequent figures relating to the proportions of employees employed in various groups of industries have been estimated from NES sampling data and refer to April 1976.

19. Figures for average male earnings by industry from NES (1976), op.cit., Part C, Tables 54 and 55.

20. Figures for average female earnings by industry from NES (1976), op.cit., Part C, Tables 56 and 57.

21. Figures calculated from Royal Commission, op.cit., Table M.10, p. 263.

22. NBPI (1971), op.cit., Appendix B, pp. 157-166.

23. J.R. Crossley, Collective Bargaining, Wage Structure, Labour Market, in E.M. Hugh-Jones (ed), Wage Structure in Theory and Practice, North Holland, 1966.

24. This evidence was drawn primarily from the work of G.C. Routh, Occupation and Pay in Great Britain, 1906-1960, Cambridge University Press, 1965; and K.G.J.C. Knowles and D.J. Robertson, Differences between the wages of skilled and unskilled workers, 1880-1950, Bulletin of the Oxford Institute of Statistics, 1951.

For later years (1960-1970) information was obtained from Department of Employment Gazettes.

25. Figures from F. Field, What is meant by low wages?, in F. Field (ed), Are Low Wages Inevitable?, Spokesman Books, 1976, Table 1, p. 15.
26. NBPI (1971), op.cit., para. 31.
27. TURU, Equal Pay: a critical review of progress, Technical Note 26, TURU, February 1975, p. 7.
28. C. Thomas, Below Par: Women and Work, Low Pay Bulletin No. 14, Low Pay Unit, April 1977, Table 2, p. 4.
29. Reported in Royal Commission, op.cit., para. 3.64.
30. Figure from D. Jackson, H.A. Turner and F. Wilkinson, Do Trade Unions Cause Inflation?, Cambridge University Press, 1975 (2nd edition), Table 3, p. 67. The figure refers to the growth of earnings net of tax and national insurance, and adjusted for the effects of inflation.
31. For example, Abel-Smith and Townsend calculated that out of all individuals who belonged to poor families in 1960, 35% belonged to families whose income was derived solely from earnings. A family was defined as poor if its net disposable income fell below 140% of the National Assistance Scales applicable to its size and composition. B. Abel-Smith and P. Townsend, The Poor and the Poorest, Bell, 1965, Table 18, p. 42.
32. P. Townsend, Poverty as Relative Deprivation, in D. Wedderburn (ed), Poverty, Inequality and Class Structure, Cambridge University Press, 1974; P. Townsend (1979), op.cit., Chapter I.
33. The Commission classified families according to 'family units' as defined for the purposes of the Blue Book National Income and Expenditure Accounts.
34. It may be noted, however, that the use of equivalence scales is a matter of some controversy. Indeed, the Commission itself acknowledged that the plausibility of the assumptions underlying the construction and application of the scales is inversely related to their ease of computation. The ages of children, for example, would require to be considered in producing estimates of comparable family living standards which were entirely valid, as would differences in socially determined expenditure patterns between family units. For a discussion of the problems involved, see P. Townsend (1979) op.cit., pp. 262-67. The Commission found, however, that the use of scales of varying complexity produced similar results, and on this basis, it is assumed in what follows that the Commission's results represent a more accurate account of the relation of low pay to poverty than would have been obtained had unadjusted family income been the basis for comparisons.
35. The information is summarised from paras. 2.36 to 2.46 and Tables H.11, H.12 and H.13 of the Commission's Report.
36. FIS was introduced in August 1971 and is payable to families with children where the parent is in full-time employment and where the family's income from all sources is below a specified amount. The payment normally comprises half the difference between the FIS income threshold and actual income. In 1976, the FIS qualifying threshold was £31.50 for a single child family rising

126.

by £3.50 for each additional child. Payments were subject to a maximum of £7 for families with one child rising by 50p for each additional child. The scheme is administered by the Supplementary Benefits Commission on a means-test basis.

37. Figures from Royal Commission, op.cit., Table 4.2, p. 85.
38. C. Pond, Soaking the Poor, Low Pay Bulletin No. 19, Low Pay Unit, February 1978, p. 4.
39. ibid.,
40. The household unit differs from the family unit in that the members of households are not necessarily related by blood or marriage. For the purposes of FES surveys, households comprise one or a group of people living at the same address, having meals together and with common housekeeping.
41. Low Pay Bulletin No. 1, op.cit., p. 4. More recent figures confirm this trend. Between January 1974 and January 1980, food increased by 145%, housing by 137% and fuel by 177% in comparison with an increase of 116% in durable household goods.
42. Details of the construction of the LPPI were obtained from the Low Pay Unit. The figures quoted are taken from Incomes Data Studies, Report 283, June 1978, p. 27.
43. K. Coates and R. Silburn, Poverty: the Forgotten Englishman, Penguin, 1973, p. 212.
44. A.B. Atkinson, Low Pay and the Cycle of Poverty, in F. Field (ed), Low Pay, Arrow, 1973, pp. 101-117. Lower paid manual men were defined as those with weekly earnings below two-thirds of the median earnings of adult full-time men (manual and non-manual).

Chapter 3

1. NBPI (1971), op.cit., para. 109.
2. J. Marquand, Which are the lower paid workers?, British Journal of Industrial Relations, November 1967, pp. 359-74.
3. For the purposes of this chapter, 'service industries' include the following: transport and communication; the distributive trades; insurance, banking and finance; professional and scientific services; miscellaneous services; and public administration and defence (i.e. Orders XXII to XXVII of SIC 1968).
4. Business Monitor PA1002, Report on the Census of Production 1972, Summary Tables, Department of Industry, HMSO, 1977, Table 3. Only in clothing and footwear were average earnings lower.
5. Figures calculated from Department of Employment Gazette, December 1977, pp. 1355-57.
6. Report of the Committee of Inquiry on Small Firms, J.E. Bolton, (Chairman), Cmnd. 4811, HMSO, 1971, para. 2.39.
7. The Bolton Report defined small manufacturing firms as 'enterprises' employing less than 200 workers. The enterprise classification differs from the establishment classification. An enterprise refers to a unit with ultimate control over a business whereas an establishment, as so defined in Census of Production data, is a reporting unit of a business and generally consists of more than one establishment. The Report noted, however, that there was a relatively small difference between the results of the enterprise and establishment classifications. Data on

establishments in the Census of Production are limited as in Table 3.2, to those employing more than 10 workers.

8. It may be noted that the figures in Tables 3.2 and 3.3 relating to the share of employment of small firms in the manufacturing sector differ considerably (31.9% cf 20%). This reflects the differing enterprise/establishment classifications employed and does not imply that small firms have increased in importance between 1963 and 1973. On the contrary, alternative evidence indicates that their share of employment slightly declined over this period.

9. Bolton Report (1971), op.cit., para. 1.11.

10. NBPI, Report No. 25, Pay of Workers in Agriculture in England and Wages, Cmnd. 3199, HMSO, 1967, para. 20.

11. C. Pond and S. Winyard, A profile of the low paid, in F. Field (ed), (1976), op.cit., p. 27.

12. S. Winyard, Who are the low payers?, Low Pay Bulletin No. 3, Low Pay Unit, May 1975, p. 4.

13. S.J. Prais, The Evolution of Giant Firms in Britain: 1909-1970, Cambridge University Press, 1976, Table 1.2, p. 18.

14. NBPI, Fourth General Report, Cmnd. 4093, HMSO, 1969, para. 59.

15. TUC, Low Pay - General Discussion Document, TUC, 1970, para. 10.

16. See for example, Profitability in the Pharmaceutical Industry, Merrett Cyriax Associates, 1968; A.J. Merrett and M.E. Lehr, The Private Company Today, Gower Press, 1971.

17. Reported in Economic Trends No. 169, November 1967, p. XIV, Table 1. 'Rate of return' was defined as ratio of net income to net assets.

18. Bolton Report (1971), op.cit., para. 4.18.

19. NBPI, Report No. 29, The Pay and Conditions of Manual Workers in Local Authorities, the National Health Service, Gas and Water Supply, Cmnd. 3230, HMSO, 1967.

20. Bolton Report (1971), op.cit., para. 4.19.

21. For manufacturing industries, figures calculated from Business Monitor PA1002, op.cit., Table 3. Figure for retailing calculated from Business Monitor SD22, Report on the Census of Distribution and Other Services, 1971, Part 13, Department of Industry, HMSO, 1976, Table 3.

22. A. Fels, The British Prices and Incomes Board, Occasional Paper 29, Cambridge University Press, 1972, p. 132.

23. J. Marquand (1967), op.cit., p. 367.

24. N. Bosanquet and R.J. Stephens, Another look at low pay, Journal of Social Policy, July 1972, pp. 245-252.

25. All figures calculated from Department of Employment Gazette, March 1975, op.cit.,

26. For example, H.A. Clegg, The System of Industrial Relations in Great Britain, Blackwell, 1972, p. 61.

27. Routh has shown that the share of agriculture, mining, textiles and clothing and footwear in total employment has progressively decreased since at least 1911. G. Routh (1965), op.cit., Table 18, p. 40.

28. ibid., pp. 39-42.

29. N. Bosanquet and R.J. Stephens (1972), op.cit., pp. 249-50. 'Unskilled workers' referred to those classified as such in Census

data.
30. Figures calculated from NES (1976), op.cit., Part E, Table 128.
31. Figures calculated from Department of Employment Gazette, December 1977.
32. All figures from Social Trends, No. 5, 1974, HMSO, 1974, p. 14.
33. Social Trends, No. 9, 1979, HMSO, 1978, Table 5.22, p. 93.
34. British Labour Statistics - Historical Abstract, 1886-1968, op. cit., Table 149.
35. NES (1976), op.cit., Part E, Table 137.
36. NBPI, Report No. 25 (1967), op.cit., para. 19, Table 1.
37. R. Price and G.S. Bain, Union Growth Revisited: 1947-74 in Perspective, British Journal of Industrial Relations, November 1976, pp. 339-353.
38. This figure is probably inflated owing to the exclusion of the least organised sectors. From earlier data, it is estimated that for the whole of this sector, union density in 1964 was 7%, as compared with 43% for the economy as a whole. Figures estimated from Royal Commission on Trade Unions and Employer's Associations, Selected Written Evidence, HMSO, 1968, p. 23.
39. A. Fisher and B. Dix, Low Pay and How to End it - A Union View, Pitmans, 1974, pp. 67-81.
40. Figures from NES (1976), op.cit., Part C, Tables 79, 80, 81 and 82. Figures relate to the earnings of full-time men aged 21 and over, and full-time women aged 18 and over whose pay was unaffected by absence.
41. ibid., Table 81. This is a further unusual feature of women's employment in these industries, implying some possible connection between the incidence of PBR schemes and occupational skill levels as conventionally measured.
42. NES (1968), HMSO, 1969, Table 126.
43. Where the effects of overtime are included in the calculation of drift, the measure derived is usually referred to as 'earnings drift'.
44. Royal Commission on Trade Unions and Employers' Associations 1965-1968, Lord Donovan, (Chairman), Report, Cmnd. 3623, HMSO, 1968, Appendix 5, p. 338.

Chapter 4

1. W.G. Bowen, Wage Behaviour in the Post-War Period, Princeton University, 1960, p. 70.
2. For example, A. Rees, Union Wage Gains and Enterprise Monopoly, Essays on Industrial Relations Research, University of Michigan, 1961, p. 131; H.M. Levinson, Wage Determination under Collective Bargaining, in A. Flanders (ed), Collective Bargaining, Penguin, 1971, pp. 86-118. In these and similar studies, 'wage' levels are most commonly measured in terms of male manual earnings (usually hourly) as opposed to centrally determined wage rates.
3. For example, A.M. Ross and W. Goldner, Forces affecting the inter-industry wage structure, Quarterly Journal of Economics, May 1950, pp. 254-281; W.G. Bowen (1960), op.cit., p. 91.
4. ibid., p. 91.
5. M. Segal, The Relation between Union Impact and Market Structure,

Quarterly Journal of Economics, February 1964, pp. 96-114.

6. H.M. Levinson (1971), op.cit., p. 106.

7. Bolton Report (1971), op.cit., para. 2.40, p. 21.

8. _Department of Employment Gazette_, February 1977, Table 2, pp. 114-115. 'Small firms' referred to establishments employing less than 50 workers, 'intermediate firms' to establishments employing 200 to 999 workers, and 'large firms' to establishments employing 1,000 or more workers.

9. J.H. Pencavel, Relative Wages and Trade Unions in the United Kingdom, _Economica_, May 1974, pp. 194-210.

10. Given, however, that plant bargaining is normally restricted to plants employing more than 250 workers, Pencavel's results might again simply reflect the negative influence of the small firm competitive market environment on earnings and union power as opposed to the effects of differences in bargaining arrangements.

11. J.T. Dunlop, Productivity and the Wage Structure, in R. Perlman (ed), _Wage Determination - Market or Power Forces?_, D.C. Heath, 1964, pp. 57-73.

12. W. Salter, _Productivity and Technological Change_, Cambridge University Press, 1966, pp. 114-115.

13. A. Jones, _The New Inflation_, André Deutsch, London, 1973, Chapter 3.

14. ibid., p. 21.

15. H.A. Turner and D.A.S. Jackson, On the Determination of the General Wage Level - A World Analysis; or 'Unlimited Labour Forever', _Economic Journal_, December 1970, pp. 827-49.

16. D. Robinson and I. Macfarline, Inter-industry wage relationships in Britain, 1948-69. _Paper read to SSRC labour workshop_, Mimeographed, London, 1973.

17. The Wilberforce Report, Table A, in J. Hughes and R. Moore (eds), _A Special Case? - Social Justice and the Miners_, Penguin, 1972, p. 128.

18. An application of this perspective to the British economy is contained in M.R. Fisher, _The Economic Analysis of Labour_, Weidenfield and Nicolson, 1971.

19. For example, N. Bosanquet and R.J. Stephens (1972), op.cit., A.B. Atkinson (1973), op.cit.,

20. N. Bosanquet, The Real Low Pay Problem, in F. Field (1973), op. cit., p. 26.

21. H.M. Wachtel and C. Betsey, Employment at Low Wages, _Review of Economics and Statistics_, May 1972, pp. 121-28.

22. B. Chiplin and P.J. Sloane, Sexual Discrimination in the Labour Market, _British Journal of Industrial Relations_, November 1974, pp. 371-402.

23. N. Bosanquet and P.B. Doeringer, Is There a Dual Labour Market in Great Britain?, _Economic Journal_, June 1973, pp. 421-435.

24. ibid., p. 424. The factors which determine a firm's internal manpower policy and thus give rise to market duality under this model are more fully discussed in Section 3.

25. B. Chiplin and P.J. Sloane (1974), op.cit., p. 375.

26. N. Bosanquet and P.B. Doeringer (1973), op.cit., p. 425.

27. G.C. Allen, _The Structure of Industry in Britain - A study in Economic Change_, Longmans, 1966, p. 19.

130.

28. ibid., p. 20.
29. The British economy since 1945, Economic Progress Report No. 100, HMSO, July 1978, p. 6.
30. C.T. Stewart (Jr), Low Wage Workers in an Affluent Society, Nelson Hall, 1974, Table 13, p. 75.
31. ibid., p. 78.
32. NBPI, Report No.127, Man-Made Fibre and Cotton Yarn Prices (Second Report), Cmnd. 4180, HMSO, 1969, Table 1, p. 2.
33. A. Glyn and R. Sutcliffe, British Capitalism, Workers and the Profit Squeeze, Penguin, 1972, pp. 143-47.
34. ibid., p. 127.
35. ibid., p. 144.
36. H. Braverman, Labor and Monopoly Capital, Monthly Review Press, London, 1974, pp. 302-04.
37. While the ratios of female to male employment were found to be relatively high in some low paying manufacturing industries, (textiles, leather, clothing and footwear - see Table 3.9), these industries nevertheless accounted for a very small proportion (approximately 6%) of total women in employment.
38. The low rate of turnover in public administration may reflect the relatively advantageous 'non-wage' benefits associated with public employment (e.g. pension schemes, sickness benefits, and, until recently, at least, relative job security).
39. J.E. Cairnes, Some Leading Principles of Political Economy, Macmillan, 1874.
40. For example, H. Lydall, The Structure of Earnings, Oxford University Press, 1968.
41. For example, J.K. Arrow, Models of Job Discrimination, in A.H. Pascal (ed), Racial Discrimination in Economic Life, D.C. Heath, 1972.
42. See, for example, R. Hyman and I. Brough, Social Values and Industrial Relations, Blackwell 1975 (especially Chapter 5).
43. P.B. Doeringer and M.J. Piore, Internal Labor Markets and Manpower Analysis, D.C. Heath, 1971.
44. An alternative explanation, as implied in Section 2, is that low paying manufacturing industries are presently undergoing a process of change, possible in response to international competitive pressures (pressures from which service industries are largely immune), and have increasingly been forced to adopt a high-skill, high-technology profile more characteristic of the primary sector. The decline of women from these industries and recent trends in productivity are consistent with this inter- pretation and it remains to be seen whether these changes result in the long term in relative increases in earnings.
45. H. Braverman (1974), op.cit., p. 425.
46. Braverman refers, for example, to increasing mechanisation and division of labour in retail distribution, reflecting the recent growth of supermarkets and hypermarkets, and argues that this process has largely displaced the 'all round' skills of the small shopkeeper. This development perhaps accounts for recent productivity trends in distribution, one service industry where rates of growth in productivity have recently been above average (Table 3.8).

47. J. Rubery, Structured Labour Markets, Worker Organisation and Low Pay, Cambridge Journal of Economics, No.2, March 1978, pp. 17-36.
48. Social Trends No. 10, 1980, HMSO, 1979, Chart 7.12, p. 166.
49. Figures estimated from Social Trends No. 3, 1972, HMSO, 1972, Table 148, and National Income and Expenditure Blue Book 1973, HMSO 1973, Table 1.
50. Social Trends No. 10, op.cit., p. 38.
51. E.J. Hobsbawm, Industry and Empire, Pelican, 1975, p. 245.
52. F. Parkin, Class Inequality and Political Order, Paladin, 1971, p. 125.
53. D. Yaffe, The Crisis of Profitability: a critique of the Glyn and Sutcliffe Thesis, New Left Review, No. 80, July-August 1973, pp. 45-59.
54. Yaffe notes that it was in those industries where investment was greatest (e.g. steel, shipbuilding, mining) rather than least, which experienced the sharpest reductions in employment. This coincides with the findings of the previous chapter. The tendency for investment to displace, rather than re-employ labour at a certain stage of capital accumulation is attributed to the tendency for the 'rate of profit' (roughly corresponding to the rate of return on capital employed) to fall, owing to a rise in the 'organic composition of capital' (roughly the capital/labour ratio). Yaffe argues that it is the attempts of industry to offset this tendency through mergers and the expansion of markets across national boundaries which explain the recent intensification of international competition, rather than as Glyn and Sutcliffe have argued, that the intensification of international competition has caused profit rates to fall.
55. Annual Abstract of Statistics, No. 113, 1976, HMSO, 1976, Table 413.
56. D. Glynn, Is Government Borrowing Too High?, Lloyds Bank Review, No. 122, October 1976, p. 20.
57. Figures from M. Stone, Gimme Shelter!, in U.S. Capitalism in Crisis, Union for Radical Political Economics, New York, 1978, p. 185.
58. The tendency for low productivity industries to 'suck in' and thereby increase their relative share of total employment has been noted by V.R. Fuchs, The Service Economy, Columbia University Press, 1968, pp. 4-5; C.T. Stewart (1974), op.cit., p. 76.
59. A description of pre-war employment trends in distribution (and miscellaneous services) is contained in G.C. Allen (1966), op.cit. pp. 7-8.
60. C.T. Stewart (1974), op.cit., p. 76.
61. General Household Survey, 1978, HMSO, 1980, Table 3.33, p. 46.
62. D. Stephen, Immigrant Workers and Low Pay, in F. Field (1973), op.cit., pp. 61-75.
63. M. Brown and S. Winyard, Low Pay in Hotels and Catering, Low Pay Pamphlet No.2, Low Pay Unit, 1975, p. 18.
64. H. Braverman (1974), op.cit., p. 384.
65. Social Indicators, 1960-75, Statistical Office of European Communities, Luxembourg, 1977, pp. 210-12.

66. N.P. Hepworth, Local Authority Expenditure, in The Three Banks Review, No. 127, September 1980, p. 17.

67. DHSS, Priorities for Health and Personal Social Services, HMSO, 1976, para. 2.1.

68. Stephen argues that the reliance on foreign labour to man public services in the 1950s and 1960s also indicates government attempts to restrict the growth of wage costs and public expenditure. Though labour markets were then tight, Stephen notes that a number of British regions continued to experience fairly high levels of unemployment. However, the costs of attracting domestic labour to the depressed Inner London Boroughs (Camden, Lambeth) and to other areas where it was needed were, in terms of wages and improvements to housing, congestion and the quality of life generally, higher than the costs of relying on immigrant labour which was more prepared to endure low wages and poor living conditions. D. Stephen (1973), op.cit., pp. 70-71.

69. J. Rubery (1978), op.cit., p. 28.

70. Braverman cites the evidence of Fuchs (V.R. Fuchs (1968), op.cit.,) which showed that from 1930, the average earnings of service workers in America (men and women combined) slipped 'with remarkable consistency' further behind those of workers in the industry sector so that by 1959, industry earnings were on average 17% higher. Thereafter, the gap continued to widen. Moreover, through multi-regressional analysis, Fuchs found that this growing gap in earnings was not fully accounted for by changes in the occupational composition of each sector in terms of race, age, sex or education. These changes 'explained' only about one-half of the growing spread in pay. H. Braverman (1974), op.cit., pp. 394-395.

71. ibid., p. 384.

72. N. Bosanquet (1973), op.cit., p. 25.

73. The relative importance of PBR in low paying manufacturing industries possibly reflects the greater need for flexibility of production in those export industries most vulnerable to international competition and thus prone to wide fluctuations in product demand. In the boot and shoe trade, for example, McCormick notes that the piecework system in operation has proved 'eminently suitable' to cope with the industry's frequent bouts of short-time working. B.J. McCormick, Methods of Wage Payment, Wages Structures and the Influence of Factor and Product Markets, British Journal of Industrial Relations, July 1977, pp. 246-63.

74. October 1966 figures from NBPI, Report No. 29 (1967), op.cit., paras. 29-34; April 1976 figures from NES (1976), op.cit., Part C, Table 79.

75. B.J. McCormick (1977), op.cit., p. 253.

76. H.F. Lydall, Inflation and the Earnings Gap, in B.J. McCormick and E. Owen Smith (eds), The Labour Market, Penguin, 1968, pp. 320-346.

Chapter 5

1. E.J. Hobsbawm (1975), op.cit., p. 284.
2. Statement on the Economic Considerations affecting relations between Employers and Workers, Cmnd. 7018, HMSO, 1947.
3. TUC, Report No. 79, 1947, p. 219.
4. Statement on Personal Incomes, Costs and Prices, Cmnd. 7321, HMSO, 1948, para. 8.
5. ibid., para. 7(d).
6. TUC, Report No. 80, 1948, pp. 290-91 and sequence. Further conditions stipulated were that: the system of collective bargaining and free negotiations should remain unimpaired; that employers should limit their dividends; and that the Government should pursue a policy not only to stabilize, but to reduce prices and profits.
7. A. Flanders, Trade Unions, Hutchinson, 1970, p. 109.
8. ibid.,
9. H. Pelling, A History of British Trade Unionism, Pelican, 1971, p. 226.
10. W.G. Runciman, Relative Deprivation and Social Justice, Routledge and Kegan Paul, 1966, p. 91.
11. H. Pelling (1971), op.cit., p. 235.
12. Cited in A. Flanders (1970), op.cit., p. 111.
13. H. Pelling (1971), op.cit., p. 236.
14. A. Flanders (1970), op.cit., p. 112.
15. H. Pelling (1971), op.cit., p. 235.
16. A. Flanders (1970), op.cit., pp. 113-14.
17. Incomes Policy, The Next Step, Cmnd. 1626, HMSO, 1962, para. 7.
18. National Incomes Commission, Cmnd. 1844, HMSO, 1962, para. 6.
19. TUC, Report No. 94, 1962, Appendix A, para. 9.
20. A. Flanders (1971), op.cit., p. 116.
21. R. Hyman and I. Brough (1975), op.cit., pp. 98-107.
22. Joint Statement of Intent on Productivity, Prices and Incomes, House of Commons Debates, Fifth Series, Vol. 704, 1964, Col. 385-388.
23. Prices and Incomes Policy, Cmnd. 2639, HMSO, 1965, para. 15.
24. Prices and Incomes Standstill: Period of Severe Restraint, Cmnd. 3150, HMSO, 1966, para. 28.
25. For example, NBPI, Report No. 17, Wages in the Bakery Industry, Cmnd. 3019, HMSO, 1966; NBPI, Report No. 25 (1967), op.cit., (i.e. agricultural workers); NBPI, Report No. 27, Pay of Retail Drapery, Outfitting and Footwear Trades Workers, Cmnd. 3224, HMSO, 1967; NBPI, Report No. 29 (1967), op.cit., (i.e. NHS, local authority manual workers); NBPI, Report No. 48, Charges, Costs and Wages in the Road Haulage Industry, Cmnd. 3482, HMSO, 1967.
26. Cited in A. Fisher and B. Dix (1974), op.cit., p. 40.
27. C. Trinder, Living Standards of People at Work, in M. Young (ed), Poverty Report 1975: A Report of the Institute of Community Studies, Temple Smith, 1975. Hyman and Brough argue, on the other hand, that a number of Conservative policies implemented in this period were overtly 'orientated towards inequality'. Various tax changes, for example, were specially favourable to the highest income groups; and the Review Body on Top Salaries set up by the

Government allowed increases of up to £2,500 a year for those in the top earnings brackets. R. Hyman and I. Brough (1975), op.cit. p. 104.

28. TUC, Collective Bargaining and the Social Contract, TUC, 26th June, 1974, para. 34. Priority was also to be given to negotiating agreements which had beneficial effects on unit costs; which improved non-wage benefits such as holiday and sick pay and pensions; and which worked towards the elimination of pay discrimination, especially among women.

29. The Attack on Inflation after 31st July 1977, Cmnd. 6882, HMSO, July 1977, para. 14.

30. Winning the Battle Against Inflation, Cmnd. 7293, HMSO, July 1978, para. 17.

31. A. Fisher and B. Dix (1974), op.cit., p. 19.

32. TUC, Report No. 98, 1966, p. 326.

33. ibid., p. 461.

34. At the 1977 Congress, however, a resolution moved by Alan Fisher to raise the 1974 £30 target to £50 was rejected, largely on the recommendation of Len Murray. Speaking against the motion, Murray argued that the adoption of minimum targets would be contrary to a return to orderly collective bargaining, in that it would impose a commitment on negotiators who may have 'alternative priorities'. He also argued that the £50 target could be inflationary and that the 'biggest way' to assist the low paid was through containing prices. TUC, Report No. 109, 1977, pp. 516-18.

35. T. Cliff, The Crisis: Social Contract or Socialism, Pluto Press, 1975, pp. 47-48.

36. The series of Economic Reviews published by the TUC from 1968 followed the decision of the General Council in 1967 to develop its own incomes policy as an alternative to the statutory policies of the Government which were provoking increasing trade union opposition. There was strong pressure for this move from the TGWU. The 1968 Review proposed an annual increase in money wages of 14/- a week, a formula deliberately chosen (instead of the $3\frac{1}{2}$% norm then being considered by Government) to favour the low paid. However, this was approved by a slender majority only at a subsequent conference of trade union executives.

37. TUC (1970), op.cit.,

38. TUC, Strategy for Low Pay, Review of Collective Bargaining Developments, No. 1, TUC, 1972.

39. Hyman and Brough note certain similarities in the industrial relations climate of the late 1940s and mid-1960s. In 1948, the notion of incomes policy as an instrument of social justice had found many influential advocates, including Barbara Wootton who published proposals to this effect. (B. Wootton, The Social Foundations of Wages Policy, Allen and Unwin, 1962 (first published in 1955). Indeed, Wootton suggested that the 1948 White Paper, with its exclusive emphasis on 'old-fashioned economic criteria' was 'out of harmony with the mood of the times'. A similar argument was outlined by Flanders in a Fabian Pamphlet published with trade union support. (A. Flanders, A Policy for Real Wages, Fabian Society, 1950). Cited in R. Hyman and I. Brough (1975), op.cit., p. 99.

40. ibid., p. 106.
41. K. Coates and R. Silburn (1970), op.cit., p. 13.
42. ibid., p. 15.
43. For example, R.M. Titmuss, Income Distribution and Social Change, Allen and Unwin, 1962.
44. Ministry of Social Security, Circumstances of Families, HMSO, 1967.
45. TUC, Report No. 99, 1967, pp. 509-10. Motion moved by Mr W.C. Anderson (NALGO).
46. As source to Table 5.1, p. 3.
47. TUC (1970), op.cit., para. 2.
48. ibid.,
49. Productivity, Prices and Incomes Policy After 1969, Cmnd. 4237, HMSO, 1969, para. 72.
50. T. Cliff (1975), op.cit., p. 48; T. Cliff, The Employers' Offensive, Pluto Press, 1970, p. 209.

Chapter 6

1. J. Edmonds and G. Radice, Low Pay, Fabian Research Series 270, Fabian Society, 1968, p. 3.
2. A. Fisher and B. Dix (1974), op.cit., p. 4.
3. For example, the 1970 discussion document considered the lowest decile criterion, the two-thirds average earnings criterion (both criteria applied to the male manual earnings distribution), and the Supplementary Benefits formula, and concluded that 'there is no reason in principle why any of these methods should be preferred to any other, and it would probably be appropriate to take them all into account in arriving at a figure'. TUC (1970), op.cit., para. 73. The levels of minimum wage targets adopted by the TUC since 1967 were justified in successive Economic Reviews according to both the two-thirds average criterion and the Supplementary Benefits formula.
4. This sort of argument was used, for example, in the 1970 TUC document when discussing the national minimum wage proposal and methods of eliminating low pay from wages council sectors.
5. W.G. Runciman (1966), op.cit., p. 251. Perhaps, however, the notion of poverty as a purely relative phenomenon has been over-emphasised in recent academic work, in that an obvious retort to the question posed is that ill health and death are more likely to result from an inadequate diet than an inadequate education. Moreover, some of the more 'universal' consequences of poverty as traditionally defined (incidence of rickets and other diet-deficiency diseases, insanitary and overcrowded living conditions, hypothermia) are by no means unknown in Britain and it would be somewhat arrogant to argue that trade unions are necessarily 'wrong' or 'illogical' in demanding or agreeing upon a minimum standard of living for all in the absence of a simultaneous demand for a substantial redistribution of income.
6. B. Wootton (1962), op.cit., p. 110.
7. Incomes Policy - Report of a Conference of Executive Committees of Affiliated Organisations, TUC, 1967, para. 117.
8. TUC (1972), op.cit., para. 2. (Strategy for Low Pay).

136.

9. R. Hyman and I. Brough (1975), op.cit., p. 223.
10. Figures estimated from Department of Employment Gazette, October 1978.
11. In many cases, however, the employment structure of the bargaining unit is a constraining factor. In discussing this approach with an official of NALGO, it was pointed out that since the overwhelming majority of white-collar staff in the NHS and local government are employed at the lower end of incremental scales, no appreciable increase in the earnings of the lower paid could result from restraint by higher paid workers.
12. T. Cliff (1975), op.cit., p. 56.
13. C. Trinder (1975), op.cit., p. 35. These threshold payments were first introduced as part of the Heath Government's pay policy as a measure specifically intended to safeguard the earnings of the lower paid.
14. The £6 Trap, Low Pay Paper No. 6, Low Pay Unit, August 1975.
15. Economic Review 1971, TUC, March 1971, paras. 82-87.
16. Economic Review 1977, TUC, February 1977, paras. 212-222.
17. C. Pond et al (1976), op.cit., p. 13.
18. ibid., p. 14. (Jack Jones quote from New Statesman, January 1972; Donnet and Lipsey's response from Tribune, 24th December 1974).
19. Evidence of Michael Meacher, 'The Malaise of the Low-Paid Worker, in J. Hughes and R. Moore (1972), op.cit., pp. 92-97.
20. C. Pond et al (1976), op.cit., p. 8.
21. Initiation of campaign reported in Financial Times, 2nd January, 1967. 'Minimum Wage Level Urged'.
22. Department of Employment and Productivity, A National Minimum Wage: report of an inter-departmental working party, HMSO, 1969.
23. In Place of Strife: A Policy for Industrial Relations, Cmnd. 3888, HMSO, January 1969.
24. TUC (1970), op.cit., para. 69.
25. TUC, Report No. 102, 1970, p. 460.
26. TUC, Report No. 106, 1974, pp. 443-50. As noted previously, even the commitment to voluntary minimum targets was later dropped at the 1977 TUC.
27. A. Fisher and B. Dix (1974), op.cit., p. 102.
28. T. Cliff (1975), op.cit., p. 46.
29. For example, Y. Brozen, The Effects of Statutory Minimum Wage Increases on Teenage Employment, Journal of Law and Economics, Chicago, April 1969, pp. 109-122.
30. For example, C. St J. O'Herlihy, Measuring Minimum Wage Effect in the United States, International Labour Organisation, Mimeographed, 1969.
31. NBPI (1971), op.cit., Appendix G, para. 19. The Board did, however, note that certain countries with minimum wage legislation (e.g. Australia and New Zealand) also had a more egalitarian distribution of earnings than had Britain. The possibility of a link, however, was not discussed.
32. A. Fisher and B. Dix (1974), op.cit., (especially Chapter 6). The ability of social democratic governments to achieve fundamental reforms in the distribution of income and wealth by parliamentary means is, of course, questionable, and has been adequately discussed elsewhere. See, for example, R. Miliband, Parliamentary

Socialism, Merlin, 1964; R. Miliband, _The State in Capitalist Society_, Weidenfield and Nicolson, 1969; F. Parkin (1971), op.cit.,
33. TUC (1970), op.cit., para. 75.
34. See, for example, _Economic Policy and Collective Bargaining in 1973_, TUC, March 1973, para. 105.
35. A. Fisher and B. Dix (1974), op.cit., p. 81.
36. R. Moore, Can't the trade unions do more?, in F. Field (ed) (1976), op.cit., pp. 105-117.
37. Economic Review 1971, op.cit., para. 29.
38. A. Fels (1972), op.cit., p. 131.
39. See, for example, _Collective Bargaining and Trade Union Development in Wages Councils Sector_, TUC, March 1969, paras. 58-72; TUC (1970), op.cit., para. 47.
40. The Act changed existing procedures in five main ways: wages councils are now permitted to make their own wage regulation Orders and decide the operative date; councils can fix other terms and conditions besides wages and holidays; trade unions and employers can appoint their own members to wages councils; trade unions can apply to convert a wages council to a statutory joint industrial council which contains no independent members, a measure designed to give both sides in a wages council some practice at setting wages in a semi-voluntary setting; and Schedule 11 of the Act, which replaced Section 8 of the 1959 Act, now allows unions to use the ACAS machinery to force an employer covered by a council to recognise the terms and conditions that the union has already negotiated with other employers in the industry.
41. TUC (March 1969), op.cit., (Report of Proceedings), pp. 24-64.
42. TUC _Report No. 102, 1970_, p. 461.
43. See Axing Low Pay, _Low Pay Paper No. 9_, Low Pay Unit, February 1976, p. 5.
44. TUC (1972), op.cit., (Strategy for Low Pay), paras. 16-17.
45. Low Pay Unit (February 1976), op.cit., p. 6.
46. J. Jenning and P. Brown, _The Boxmakers_, SOGAT, 1976.
47. S. Winyard, Whither Wages Councils?, Low Pay Unit (March 1975), op.cit., p. 1.
48. Low Pay Unit (February 1976), op.cit., p. 8.
49. C. Craig, J. Rubery, R. Tarling and F. Wilkinson, Abolition and after: the Paper Box Wages Council, _Research Paper No. 12_, Department of Employment, June 1980.
50. ibid., p. 87.
51. N. Bosanquet, Can we protect the very low paid?, in F. Field (ed), (1976), op.cit., pp. 125-135.
52. R. Price and G.S. Bain (1976), op.cit., Table 3, pp. 342-43.
53. Figures estimated from Statistical Supplements to TUC Reports, 1965, 1969 and 1976.

Postscript

1. _Department of Employment Gazette_, December 1980, Table 2.2.

BIBLIOGRAPHY

ABEL-SMITH, B & TOWNSEND, P   The Poor and the Poorest, Bell, 1965.

ALLEN, G C   The Structure of Industry in Britain - A Study in Economic Change, Longmans, 1966.

ARROW, J K   Models of Job Discrimination, in Pascal, A.H. (ed), Racial Discrimination in Economic Life, D.C. Heath, 1972.

ATKINSON, A B   Low Pay and the Cycle of Poverty, in Field, F. (ed), Low Pay, Arrow, 1973.

BEHREND, H   What is Lower Pay? - 1971 (follow-up survey, SSRC Newsletter 12, SSRC, June 1971.

BEHREND, H   Attitudes to Price Increases and Pay Claims, NEDO Monograph 4, NEDO, 1974.

BEHREND, H & KNOWLES, A   What is meant by lower pay? SSRC Newsletter 8, SSRC, March 1970.

BEHREND, H, KNOWLES, A & DAVIES, J   Views on Pay Increases, Fringe Benefits and Low Pay, Economic and Social Research Institute Paper No. 56, Dublin, August 1970.

BOSANQUET, N   The Real Low Pay Problem, in Field, F (ed), Low Pay, Arrow, 1973.

BOSANQUET, N   Can we protect the very low paid? in Field, F (ed), Are Low Wages Inevitable? Spokesman Books, 1976.

139

140.

BOSANQUET, N & DOERINGER, P B	Is There a Dual Labour Market in Great Britain? Economic Journal, June 1973.
BOSANQUET, N & STEPHENS, R J	Another look at low pay, Journal of Social Policy, July 1972.
BOWEN, W G	Wage Behaviour in the Post-War Period, Princeton University, 1960.
BRAVERMAN, H	Labor and Monopoly Capital, Monthly Review Press, London, 1974.
BROWN, M & WINYARD, S	Low Pay in Hotels and Catering, Low Pay Pamphlet No. 2, Low Pay Unit, 1975.
BROZEN, Y	The Effects of Statutory Minimum Wage Increases on Teenage Employment, Journal of Law and Economics, Chicago, April 1969.
CAIRNES, J E	Some Leading Principles of Political Economy, Macmillan, 1874.
CENTRAL STATISTICAL OFFICE	Standard Industrial Classification 1968, HMSO, 1968.
CENTRAL STATISTICAL OFFICE	Annual Abstract of Statistics, No.113, 1976, HMSO, 1976.
CENTRAL STATISTICAL OFFICE	National Income and Expenditure Blue Book 1973, HMSO, 1973.
CHIPLIN, B & SLOANE, P J	Sexual Discrimination in the Labour Market, British Journal of Industrial Relations, November 1974.
CLEGG, H A	The System of Industrial Relations in Great Britain, Blackwell, 1972.
CLIFF, T	The Employers' Offensive, Pluto Press, 1970.
CLIFF, T	The Crisis: Social Contract or Socialism, Pluto Press, 1975.
COATES, K & SILBURN, R	Poverty: the Forgotten Englishman, Penguin, 1973.
COUNTER INFORMATION SERVICES	Women under attack: CIS Special Report, Counter Information Services, 1976.

CRAIG, C, RUBERY, J,
TARLING, R & WILKINSON, F

Abolition and after: the Paper Box
Wages Council, Research Paper No. 12,
Department of Employment, June 1980.

CRAIG, C, RUBERY, J,
TARLING, R & WILKINSON, F

Abolition and after: the Cutlery
Wages Council, Research Paper No. 18,
Department of Employment, January
1981.

CROSSLEY, J R

Collective Bargaining, Wage
Structure, Labour Market, in Hugh-
Jones, E.M. (ed), Wage Structure in
Theory and Practice, North Holland,
1966.

DEPARTMENT OF EMPLOYMENT

British Labour Statistics -
Historical Abstract, 1886-1968,
HMSO, 1971.

DEPARTMENT OF EMPLOYMENT
GAZETTE

July 1974
January 1975
March 1975
July 1975
September 1975
February 1976
February 1977
December 1977
October 1978
December 1980

DEPARTMENT OF EMPLOYMENT

New Earnings Survey 1976, Parts A,
C, E and F, HMSO, 1976-77.

DEPARTMENT OF EMPLOYMENT

New Earnings Survey 1980, Part C,
December 1980.

DEPARTMENT OF EMPLOYMENT
AND PRODUCTIVITY

Employment and Productivity Gazette,
December 1968.

DEPARTMENT OF EMPLOYMENT
AND PRODUCTIVITY

New Earnings Survey 1968, HMSO, 1969.

DEPARTMENT OF EMPLOYMENT
AND PRODUCTIVITY

A National Minimum Wage: report of
an inter-departmental working party,
HMSO, 1969.

DEPARTMENT OF HEALTH AND
SOCIAL SECURITY

Priorities for Health and Personal
Social Services, HMSO, 1976.

DEPARTMENT OF INDUSTRY

Business Monitor M3, Company Finance
(Seventh Issue), Central Statistical
Office (CSO), HMSO, 1976.

142.

DEPARTMENT OF INDUSTRY — Business Monitor SD22, Report on the Census of Distribution and Other Services, 1971, Part 13, CSO, HMSO, 1976.

DEPARTMENT OF INDUSTRY — Business Monitor PA1003, Analysis of UK manufacturing (local) units by employment size (1973), CSO, HMSO, 1976.

DEPARTMENT OF INDUSTRY — Business Monitor PA1002, Report on the Census of Production 1972, Summary Tables, CSO, HMSO, 1977.

DEPARTMENT OF INDUSTRY — Business Monitor PA1000, Census of Production 1978, Provisional Results, CSO, HMSO, 1980.

DOERINGER, P B & PIORE, M J — Internal Labor Markets and Manpower Analysis, D.C. Heath, 1971.

DUNLOP, J T — Productivity and the Wage Structure, in Perlman, R. (ed), Wage Determination – Market or Power Forces? D.C. Heath, 1964.

ECONOMIC PROGRESS REPORT No. 100 — The British Economy since 1945, HMSO, July 1978.

ECONOMIC TRENDS No. 169 — CSO, HMSO, November 1967.

EDMONDS, J & RADICE, G — Low Pay, Fabian Research Series 270, Fabian Society, 1968.

FELS, A — The British Prices and Incomes Board, Occasional Paper 29, Cambridge University Press, 1972.

FIELD, F — What is meant by low wages? in Field, F (ed), Are Low Wages Inevitable? Spokesman Books, 1976.

FISHER, M R — The Economic Analysis of Labour, Weidenfeld and Nicolson, 1971.

FISHER, A & DIX, B — Low Pay and How to End it – A Union View, Pitmans, 1974.

FLANDERS, A — Trade Unions, Hutchinson, 1970.

FUCHS, V R — The Service Economy, Columbia University Press, 1968.

GENERAL HOUSEHOLD SURVEY 1978   HMSO, 1980.

GLYN, A & SUTCLIFFE, R — British Capitalism, Workers and the Profit Squeeze, Penguin, 1972.

GLYNN, D — Is Government Borrowing Too High? Lloyds Bank Review No. 122, October 1976.

HEPWORTH, N P — Local Authority Expenditure, The Three Banks Review No. 127, September 1980.

HOBSBAWM, E J — Industry and Empire, Pelican, 1975.

HOUSE OF COMMONS DEBATES — Joint Statement of Intent on Productivity, Prices and Incomes, Fifth Series, Vol.704, 1964.

HUGHES, J — What part can a minimum wage play? in Field, F (ed), Are Low Wages Inevitable? Spokesman Books, 1976.

HUGHES, J & MOORE, R (eds) — A Special Case? - Social Justice and the Miners, Penguin, 1972.

HYMAN, R & BROUGH, I — Social Values and Industrial Relations, Blackwell, 1975.

INCOME DATA STUDIES — Report 283, June 1978.

INCOMES POLICY, THE NEXT STEP — Cmnd. 1626, HMSO, 1962.

IN PLACE OF STRIFE : A POLICY FOR INDUSTRIAL RELATIONS — Cmnd. 3888, HMSO, 1969.

JACKSON, D, TURNER, H A & WILKINSON, F — Do Trade Unions Cause Inflation? Cambridge University Press, 1975 (2nd edition).

JENNING, J & BROWN, P — The Boxmakers, SOGAT, 1976

JONES, A — The New Inflation, André Deutsch, London, 1973.

KNOWLES, K G J C & ROBERTSON, D J — Differences between the wages of skilled and unskilled workers, 1180-1950, Bulletin of the Oxford Institute of Statistics, 1951.

144.

LEVINSON, H M — Wage Determination under Collective Bargaining, in Flanders, A (ed), Collective Bargaining, Penguin, 1971.

LOW PAY UNIT — Low Pay Bulletins, Nos. 1, 2, 3, 14, 17 and 19, Low Pay Unit, 1975-78.

LOW PAY UNIT — The £6 trap, Low Pay Paper No. 6, Low Pay Unit, August 1975.

LOW PAY UNIT — Axing Low Pay, Low Pay Paper No. 9, Low Pay Unit, February 1976.

LYDALL, H F — Inflation and the Earnings Gap, in McCormick, B.J. and Owen Smith, E (eds), The Labour Market, Penguin, 1968.

LYDALL, H F — The Structure of Earnings, Oxford University Press, 1968.

MARQUAND, J — Which are the lower paid workers? British Journal of Industrial Relations, November 1967.

MEACHER, M — The Malaise of the Low-Paid Worker, in Hughes, J and Moore, E (eds), A Special Case? - Social Justice and the Miners, Penguin, 1972.

MERRETT CYRIAX ASSOCIATES — Profitability in the Pharmaceutical Industry, 1968.

MERRETT, A J & LEHR, M E — The Private Company Today, Gower Press, 1971.

MILIBAND, R — Parliamentary Socialism, Merlin, 1964.

MILIBAND, R — The State in Capitalist Society, Weidenfield and Nicolson, 1969.

MINISTRY OF SOCIAL SECURITY — Circumstances of Families, HMSO, 1967.

MOORE, R — Can't the trade unions do more? in Field, F (ed), Are Low Wages Inevitable? Spokesman Books, 1976.

McCORMICK, B J	Methods of Wage Payment, Wages Structures and the Influence of Factor and Product Markets, <u>British Journal of Industrial Relations</u>, July 1977.
NATIONAL BOARD FOR PRICES AND INCOMES (NBPI)	<u>Report No. 17</u>, Wages in the Bakery Industry, Cmnd. 3019, HMSO, 1966.
NATIONAL BOARD FOR PRICES AND INCOMES	<u>Report No. 25</u>, Pay of Workers in Agriculture in England and Wales, Cmnd. 3199, HMSO, 1967.
NATIONAL BOARD FOR PRICES AND INCOMES	<u>Report No. 27</u>, Pay of Retail Drapery, Outfitting and Footwear Trades Workers, Cmnd. 3224, HMSO, 1967.
NATIONAL BOARD FOR PRICES AND INCOMES	<u>Report No. 29</u>, The Pay and Conditions of Manual Workers in Local Authorities, the National Health Service, Gas and Water Supply, Cmnd. 3230, 1967.
NATIONAL BOARD FOR PRICES AND INCOMES	<u>Report No. 48</u>, Charges, Costs and Wages in the Road Haulage Industry, Cmnd. 3482, HMSO, 1967.
NATIONAL BOARD FOR PRICES AND INCOMES	<u>Fourth General Report</u>, Cmnd. 4093, HMSO, 1969.
NATIONAL BOARD FOR PRICES AND INCOMES	<u>Report No. 127</u>, Man-Made Fibre and Cotton Yarn Prices (Second Report), Cmnd. 4180, HMSO, 1969.
NATIONAL BOARD FOR PRICES AND INCOMES	<u>Report No. 169</u>, General Problems of Low Pay, Cmnd. 4648, HMSO, 1971.
NATIONAL INCOMES COMMISSION	Cmnd. 1844, HMSO, 1962.
NATIONAL INSTITUTE OF ECONOMIC AND SOCIAL RESEARCH	<u>National Institute Economic Review No. 71</u>, February 1975.
OFFICE OF MANPOWER ECONOMICS	<u>Wage Drift: Review of Literature and Research</u>, HMSO, 1973.
O'HERLIHY, C St. J	<u>Measuring Minimum Wage Effect in the US</u>, International Labour Organisation, Mimeographed, 1969.
PARKIN, F	<u>Class Inequality and Political Order</u>, Paladin, 1971.

146.

PELLING, H — A History of British Trade Unionism, Pelican, 1971.

PENCAVEL, J H — Relative Wages and Trade Unions in the United Kingdom, Economica, May 1974.

POND, C — Soaking the Poor, Low Pay Bulletin No. 19, Low Pay Unit, February 1978.

POND, C, FIELD, F & WINYARD, S — Trade Unions and Taxation, Studies for Trade Unionists, Vol.2, No.6, Workers Educational Association, 1976.

POND, C & WINYARD, S — A profile of the low paid, in Field, F (ed), Are Low Wages Inevitable? Spokesman Books, 1976.

PRAIS, S J — The Evolution of Giant Firms in Britain: 1909-1970, Cambridge University Press, 1976.

PRICE, R & BAIN, G S — Union Growth Revisited: 1948-74 in Perspective, British Journal of Industrial Relations, November 1976.

PRICES AND INCOMES POLICY — Cmnd. 2639, HMSO, 1965.

PRICES AND INCOMES STANDSTILL PERIOD OF SEVERE RESTRAINT — Cmnd. 3150, HMSO, 1966.

PRODUCTIVITY, PRICES AND INCOMES POLICY AFTER 1969 — Cmnd. 4237, HMSO, 1969.

REES, A — Union Gains and Enterprise Monopoly, Essays on Industrial Relations Research, University of Michigan, 1961.

REPORT OF THE COMMITTEE OF INQUIRY ON SMALL FIRMS (BOLTON, J E - CHAIRMAN) — Cmnd. 4811, HMSO, 1971.

ROBINSON, D & MACFARLINE, I — Inter-industry wage relationships in Britain, 1948-69, Paper read to an SSRC Labour Workshop, Mimeographed, London, 1973.

ROSS, A M & GOLDNER, W — Forces affecting the inter-industry wage structure, Quarterly Journal of Economics, May 1958.

ROUTH, G C | Occupation and Pay in Great Britain, 1906-1960, Cambridge University Press, 1965.

ROYAL COMMISSION ON THE DISTRIBUTION OF INCOME AND WEALTH REPORT No. 6 LOWER INCOMES | Cmnd. 7175, HMSO, 1978.

ROYAL COMMISSION ON TRADE UNIONS AND EMPLOYERS' ASSOCIATIONS 1965-68 (LORD DONOVAN - CHAIRMAN) REPORT | Cmnd. 3623, HMSO, 1968.

ROYAL COMMISSION ON TRADE UNIONS AND EMPLOYERS' ASSOCIATIONS | Selected Written Evidence, HMSO, 1968.

RUBERY, J | Structured labour markets, worker organisation and low pay, Cambridge Journal of Economics, No.2, March 1978.

RUNCIMAN, W G | Relative Deprivation and Social Justice, Routledge and Kegan Paul, 1966.

SALTER, W | Productivity and Technological Change, Cambridge University Press, 1966.

SEGAL, M | The Relation between Union Impact and Market Structure, Quarterly Journal of Economics, February 1964.

SOCIAL INDICATORS 1960-75 | Statistical Office of European Communities, Luxembourg, 1977.

SOCIAL TRENDS No. 3, 1972 | CSO, HMSO, 1972.

SOCIAL TRENDS No. 5, 1974 | CSO, HMSO, 1974.

SOCIAL TRENDS No. 7, 1976 | CSO, HMSO, 1976.

SOCIAL TRENDS No. 9, 1979 | CSO, HMSO, 1978.

SOCIAL TRENDS No. 10, 1980 | CSO, HMSO, 1979.

STATEMENT ON PERSONAL INCOMES, COSTS AND PRICES | Cmnd. 7321, HMSO, 1948.

148.

STEPHEN, D   Immigrant Workers and Low Pay, in
                               Field, F (ed), Low Pay, Arrow, 1973.

STEWART, C T (Jr)   Low Wage Workers in an Affluent
                               Society, Nelson Hall, Chicago, 1974.

STONE, M   Gimme Shelter! in US Capitalism in
                               Crisis, Union for Radical Political
                               Economics, New York, 1978.

THE ATTACK ON INFLATION   Cmnd. 6882, HMSO, 1977.
AFTER 31st JULY 1977

THE ECONOMIST   10th September 1977.

THE FINANCIAL TIMES   2nd January 1967.

THOMAS, C   Below: Women and Work, Low Pay
                               Bulletin No. 14, Low Pay Unit,
                               April 1977.

TITMUSS, R M   Income Distribution and Social
                               Change, Allen and Unwin, 1962.

TOWNSEND, P   Poverty as Relative Deprivation, in
                               Wedderburn, D (ed), Poverty,
                               Inequality and Class Structure,
                               Cambridge University Press, 1974.

TOWNSEND, P   Poverty in the UK, Penguin, 1979.

TRADE UNION RESEARCH UNIT   Equal Pay: a critical review of
                               progress, Technical Note 26, TURU,
                               February 1976.

TRADES UNION CONGRESS (TUC)   Annual Reports to Congress (and
                               Reports of Proceedings), Report
                               Nos. 79 (1947), 80 (1948), 94 (1962),
                               97 (1965), 98 (1966), 99 (1967),
                               102 (1970), 106 (1974), 108 (1976),
                               109 (1977).

TUC   Incomes Policy - Report of a
                               Conference of Executive Committees
                               of Affiliated Organisations, TUC,
                               1967.

TUC   Economic Review, TUC, January 1968.

TUC   Collective Bargaining and Trade
                               Union Development in Wages Councils
                               Sector, TUC, March 1969.

TUC — Low Pay: General Discussion Document, TUC, 1970.

TUC — Economic Review 1971, TUC, March 1971.

TUC — Strategy for Low Pay, Review of Collective Bargaining Developments No. 1, TUC, 1972.

TUC — Economic Policy and Collective Bargaining in 1973, TUC, March 1973.

TUC — Collective Bargaining and the Social Contract, TUC, June 1974.

TUC — Economic Review 1977, TUC, March 1977.

TRINDER, C — Living Standards of People at Work, in Young, M (ed), Poverty Report 1975: A Report of the Institute of Community Studies, Temple Smith, 1975.

TURNER, H A & JACKSON, D A S — On the Determination of the General Wage Level — A World Analysis; or "Unlimited Labour Forever", Economic Journal, December 1970.

WACHTEL, H M & BETSEY, C — Employment at Low Wages, Review of Economics and Statistics, May 1972.

WINNING THE BATTLE AGAINST INFLATION — Cmnd. 7293, HMSO, 1978.

WINYARD, S — Whither Wages Councils? Low Pay Bulletin No. 2, Low Pay Unit, March 1975.

WOOTTON, B — The Social Foundations of Wages Policy, Allen and Unwin, 1962.

YAFFE, D — The Crisis of Profitability: a critique of the Glyn and Sutcliffe Thesis, New Left Review No. 80, July — August 1973.